Survey Democracy

Emanuel Smikun, Ph.D.

Survey
Democracy

Participation
Complementary
to Elections

Survey Democracy

Published by AMINSO
300 Andover Street, Suite 157
Peabody, Massachusetts 01960, USA

ISBN-13: 978-1545044513

ISBN-10: 1545044511

Library of Congress Control Number: 2017906049

Contents

List of Figures

List of Tables

Introduction

Action Frame of Reference

Democracy attaches high value to every human life irrespective of social status or class. We find ways to compromise and to reconcile our differences rather than trying to eliminate the opposition. We try to elevate the poor and the weak higher, aiming at the rich and the powerful. In a narrower sense, for most people today democracy, our cherished ideal of government means primarily elections and human rights, including the right of free elections. We call it liberal democracy. This is also the way democracy is understood by the rest of the world. Yet this is not all that democracy has always been, and above all, not all that it can be.

As a form of government, democracy has been debated since ancient times. We are talking here of government as the process of decision-making in the public interest rather than as an organization of people making such decisions. There are many opinions about democracy. Philosophers and political scientists pointed out its advantages over the authoritarian forms of government such as monarchy or aristocracy. Its deficiencies are described primarily as chaos brought about by the rule of angry mobs. In today's world, political regimes in many countries aspire to democracy or at least declare that they do. Democracy has virtually become a universal model of government in the world.

This book argues for a participatory democracy that is complementary to and competitive with the representative democracy of elections. Without direct citizen participation in addition to representation the principle of people's sovereignty erodes. Elected government becomes self-serving oligarchy. Regular surveys of excessive deviations from standards of distributive social justice and rationality in collective consciousness and collective conscience is the most cost-effective and efficient way of overcoming voter apathy and achieving citizens participation in government. A standing public policy of reversing such deviations can strengthen social bonds and bring closer Lincoln's dream of government by the people. No form of participatory democracy can replace the historic gain of elections. But it can counterbalance them similar to the way lower houses of parliaments historically counterbalanced upper ones. The book lays a foundation for two-track election-and-survey democracy with an advanced methodology of survey data analysis that is based on action frame of reference.

Social conscience is one of the main ingredients in the fine art of survey data analysis as well as in government. Individual conscience is about being good to other people or, in Kant's terms, about treating them as ends in themselves rather than as means to other ends. Social conscience is our public ability to be good to groups of people, to status group and class structures. Social conscience relies on social consciousness but it goes further. Based on its awareness of conditions of diverse status groups and classes that form these social structures, it takes responsibility for them thus assuring social harmony in their relations. We care for more than just our family and friends. We are also not indifferent to other status groups either higher or lower than ours. We become concerned about the improvement of the entire social structure made up of all such groups. Durkheim called this collective or common conscience. The more recent debate between Gadamer and Habermas on critical thinking clarifies some of the issues that are fundamental to social conscience.[1]

In the debate, Gadamer was taking the position of truth that he thought could be found and defended by self-criticism of literary works and works of art as elements of cultural tradition. For Habermas, every tradition was a form of false consciousness, especially when followers of tradition insisted on their own truthfulness. To Habermas this was false ideology pure and simple. Gadamer objected that denial of self-criticism risked turning Habermas' critical theory of communication into an object of faith with detrimental consequences for social practices. Habermas responded that any discourse in the present must be protected from distorting ideological influences, including the so-called ideological self-criticism. According to Habermas, only external critique could give a basis for searching the truth. According Marx followed by

Habermas, all ideologies are forms of false consciousness when adopted separately and uncritically – unless they are critically reappraised and fused together in a new theory oriented to contemporary social concerns.

Ideologies become utopias when rather than using them as material for theory construction they are treated as describing objective reality and when attempts are made to build or promote movements aimed at institutionalizing such utopias. "Real utopias," especially the extreme ones of either left or right, substitute ready-made ideology for the laborious but necessary methods of the social sciences. They can be dangerous. As the history of the 20th century shows, in times of crisis utopias can and have been made real by seductive demagogical leaders putting them into practice by force. The falsehoods of ideology and utopia can be avoided in what Mannheim called a quest for reality.[2] As political reality can only be found in a synthesis of conflicting partisan positions, so must social science synthesize its particular ideological conceptions that must, in turn, be subjected to new, revised syntheses with the passage of time. True social consciousness can find reality only in critical amalgamations of received ideological legacies. Construction and testing of substantive social theories is better seen as part of research work separate from formal deductive ones such as those based on action frame of reference.

In physical sciences a frame of reference consists of points in space and time that allow for unequivocal evaluations of observed motion. Thus the history of geometry consists of concepts of frames of reference in space that were changing throughout the history of our civilization along with the history of navigation. The meaning of our geographic space was created by virtue of human travel and by the way we oriented ourselves in it. Our spatial orientation evolved across the ages from early empirical navigation based on the skipper's personal knowledge and experience, to navigation by the stars with compass and astrolabe, to astronomic navigation with marine chronometer and sextant, to the radio location and GPS navigation of today. Both geometry as the science of spatial measurement, and the development of numeration itself from fractions to negative and irrational to complex and finally to hypercomplex numbers closely followed this evolution of navigation.

Early empirical navigation was thought of in terms of elementary Euclidean geometry; navigation with compass and astrolabe in terms of Cartesian analytical geometry; astronomic navigation with the sextant in terms of non-Euclidean geometry (Gauss, Bolyai, Lobachevsky, Riemann, and others) that also gave rise to differential, projection and drawing geometries. Finally, modern GPS navigation is reflected in the science of topology. Each one of these methods of navigation and each historic period in the advent of new geometric ideas was characterized by its special method of co-measuring distance as quantities that determined a vessel's location in space. These methods also brought about new concepts of the number itself as resolving the differences between extensive and intensive quantities measured by the changing spatial frames of reference.[3]

The idea of social action as a similar analytical and representational frame of reference was introduced by

Talcott Parsons. Before Parsons, Max Weber discussed social action and its aspects – ends, means and orientations – but in an unstructured way and substantively rather than cognitively, i.e. without the organizing principle of a frame of reference. Durkheim implied a similar program in terms of social cohesion and coordination that followed rules of moral conduct. In fact, Durkheim's idea of social solidarity and Parsons' idea of social integration had very similar intentions. Parsons was critical of Durkheim's positivism as well as of Weber's idealism whose concept of social action was focused on interpretations of meanings but remained unstructured. Parsons proposed an action frame of reference as a social structure whose elements – actor, ends, means and conditions - impacted one another. This opened up a possibility to go beyond programmatic statements and interpret empirical observations as elements of social action whose structural relations are better understood than relations among multifarious variables extracted from collected survey data.[4] This is the possibility we want to realize here.

The unit act that defines action frame of reference will include more than the ideal of distributive social justice in changing social conditions for the better. Ideals – rather than actor - constitute a formal element of social action. Its material, substantive counterpart is a summary of prevailing social conditions that social justice and rationality are supposed to improve. Prevailing social conditions and the ideals of rationality are mediated by corresponding ends and means to those ends. Thus action frame of reference includes conditions, ideals, ends and means.

In terms of their underlying philosophical perspectives, ends and means combine properties of both idealistic and materialist aspects of action. Ends and means combine the properties of conditions and ideals of action in their interpenetration. The properties of conditions and ideals interpenetrate in ends and means by way of mutual cross-attribution. By themselves, ideals cannot account for prevailing conditions of action, and, in turn, circumstances of action will always remain unchanged so long as they do not involve ideals, and in this way, ends and means as well.

Good society is achieved when the structures of stratified status groups and classes are harmonized. Status groups and classes can be an active force by effectively influencing government policies. They can be pressure groups working through the power of organized and scientifically rigorous public opinion research. Based on this kind of analysis of survey results we can help formulate clear public policies of reversing excessive deviations of status group and class structures. These reversals will affect differentiated stress on principles of distributive social justice as well as on elements of goal- and instrumental rationality. Such policy decisions can take the form of various incentives and disincentives such as positive and negative taxation.

With this kind of analysis the public can legitimately participate in formulating legislative acts and executive branch policies. According to this idea of participatory survey democracy, policy recommendations will be designed to complement policy proposals advanced by elected officials and compete with them if necessary. Such survey democracy can serve as regularly scheduled referendums on all decisions by elected government. Above all, survey democracy can promote legislation and programs that elected government may not be interested in but that will serve the interests of social progress. Public opinion can become a tool of participatory democracy rather than a tool of elitist government and its two hardly distinguishable catch-all political parties. This idea of two-track democracy is closely related to this notion of action frame of reference.

Notes

[1] Gadamer (1985, 1988), Habermas (1979, 1985).

[2] "The attempt to escape ideological and utopian distortions is, in the last analysis, a quest for reality. [...] All the conflicting groups and classes in society seek this reality in their thought and deeds, and it is therefore no wonder that it appears to be different to each of them." (Mannheim, 1985, pp. 98, 101-102).

[3] See Smikun (2004).

[4] In this Parsons (1968) was following Whitehead's warning against the fallacy of misplaced concreteness that hypostatizes and reifies ontological presuppositions or models thus doubling reality. This was one of the major aspects in Parsons' critique of Weber, Durkheim, Pareto and Marshall in his *Structure of Social Action*. The debate about reification of abstract notions had been definitively resolved by Occam's razor.

1. Democracy, Liberal and Representative

Social scientists distinguish several different types of democratic government. Like all other cultural artifacts, the types of democracy are created by social scientists and philosophers for the purpose of structuring reality that otherwise is chaotic and confused. All types of democracy are such constructs rather than descriptions of historically real societies. They do not really exist – unless they penetrate public consciousness. Only then can people start believing that they represent reality.

Direct democracy is characterized by face-to-face deliberations. This is the democracy of town meetings that was practiced in the ancient city-state of Athens. Direct democracy of town meetings was possible in small New England towns. But present-day Salem is already too big for such a town meeting of all citizens. It can't be done. Then there came the idea of liberal democracy. It stressed civil liberties or rights such as freedom of speech, freedom of assembly, of protests and demonstrations. It emerged in the 17th and 18th centuries when people of Europe struggled for civil liberty-rights against autocratic powers. Autocratic rulers such as kings and emperors claimed their right to rule as divine, as a right given to them by God. Therefore, they claimed, they had absolute power over their subjects. Philosophers Thomas Hobbes, John Locke, and Jean-Jacques Rousseau opposed that claim. They rejected the idea of divine rights of kings. There is no such thing as divine right, they said. They proclaimed that all humans are born with certain inalienable natural rights. That included the right of free speech, freedom of assembly, and freedom of conscience.

Liberal Democracy

Liberal democracy reaffirmed these fundamental human rights, and that is why we value it today. This conflict between authoritarian rule and liberal ideas gave rise to the American Revolution and then to the French Revolution. That in turn triggered European socialist movements, and then nationalist movements that brought about World War I, the Soviet Union and Nazi Germany. All movements for freedom of speech, freedom of assembly, freedom of conscience and other such freedoms – all this is part of liberal democracy. The principle of right - or liberty - has been followed in Western civilization for three or four hundred years now. Yet our liberty-rights cannot be taken for granted. They must be constantly defended against those in power who would like to infringe upon them.

There are also many areas where freedoms may be curtailed for the sake of good taste or public safety. These are grey areas liable to raise hot debates, and there is no lack of them. For example, Does freedom of speech include pornography, or the use of four-letter words? Should there be freedom for neo-Nazi gatherings? Should deadly firearms be freely available to all? Or all kinds of firearms including assault rifles? Should abortions be allowed to anyone for any reason? Americans are divided on all these questions. In today's usage, there is nothing natural about human rights. They are won, and they still have to be defended today. Most of us take all these rights and liberties for granted. But they remain controversial and must be defended if we want to enjoy them.

Liberal democracy originated in defense of rights to oppose the rule of authoritarian powers such as monarchies. The values of freedom and the right to oppose government are still held high in most Western countries. And yet, despite all its advantages, liberal democracy has proved to be insufficient for good government. The United States is believed to be the most successful country in the world owing in part to upholding this principle of human rights but also because of its geographic isolation, the richness of its natural resources, and also because it avoided two world wars on its territory. These latter advantages may have been exhausted by now. As for our liberal democracy, it has shown limitations as a form of government.

Liberal democracy was inspired by the high philosophical ideals of the European Enlightenment. But there is a great disparity between abstract notions of freedom, equality and universal brotherhood, on the one hand, and concrete problems of real life, on the other.

What was missing was a connection to real life, something that Athenian direct democracy had. Representative democracy met this challenge by combining the best features of direct and liberal democratic models. This was achieved with the idea of government by people's elected representatives under the principle of one man, one vote. On the one hand, the institution of regular elections of people's representatives satisfies the requirement of free choice. At the same time it satisfies the requirement of equality by inclusion of all citizens irrespective of race or religion.

Representative Democracy

Representative democracy marked a huge progress in the Western world. However, like anything else in Western civilization, representative democracy is not a perfect form of government. It can be abused. Hence mistrust of our government at the present time that has been present at least since the Watergate affair. Controlled by professional political advisors, elections turn out to produce government of the elites. The effective control by the elites is facilitated by the fact that we have the highest level of income inequality in the world with the possible exception of today's Russia where oligarchy prevails. Hence the current revolt against the political establishment in the USA.

On the face of it, the United States has a democratic system of one man/woman, one vote. In reality the candidates we vote for are nominated through the system of competitive elitism in primaries that are driven mostly by money. The big banks and other powerful vested interests heavily fund both Republican and Democratic Party candidates. Max Weber's idea of party side-by-side with status and class is only relevant for a newly formed class, of a class having self-conscious ideals in the sense of identity social movements. Only such a party would have distinct class interests with a distinct social base. Such are European ideological parties as opposed to established, old parties having no distinct social base and simply trying to catch all voters relying on demagoguery and sleek election campaigns by professional marketing specialists. The two American parties – Democratic and Republican – are still seen as broadly representing lower and upper classes, respectively. This division is inherited from the Marxist theory of historic materialism, of class struggle, and may not represent true class interests today. The simple dichotomous division into upper and lower classes is too insufficient.

Until Trump came to the scene, only half of registered voters actually voted because they did not believe that their votes affected the outcome of elections. When we do vote we often vote not for the candidate we want to win, but rather against the opposing candidate. By stressing the categories of race, gender, and religion, these primordial demographic groups are pitted against each other according to the old Roman principle of divide and rule (*divide et impere*). Operating with these demographic categories only serves to divide us. Candidates use them to manipulate us and take advantage appealing to our lowest parochial instincts. Not only is this detrimental to social bonds that unite us as Americans, it also takes our attention away from what really unites us – from our aspiration for social justice. Similarly to ancient Rome we have the American Empire today that acts as a world policeman. As part of this role in the world, our government collects and keeps information on everybody. This is done in the name of democracy and human rights.

Our system of government with the president as commander-in-chief is better suited for war than for peace. Winston Churchill famously stated: "Democracy is a bad form of government except all other forms are even worse." This indicated limitations of our representative democracy. Representative democracy by elections is very important. It provides leadership by the best of us. That is the ideal. That is what this democracy should be.

Yet our democracy has certain undemocratic elements. Congressmen are elected to represent the interests of their constituents. This is the original idea of representative democracy. It is not necessarily reality. In reality, elected officials often seek personal power to promote themselves with attractive promises during election campaigns. It is widely recognized that the American system of representative democracy serves the interests of upper classes. Our liberal Constitution does allow protests and movements that are opposed to these interests. But this freedom is given only so long as the protests remain toothless and are used just to blow off the steam of public frustration. This is what happened with the Occupy movement and protests against globalization.

We also have certain elements of authoritarian rule. In national emergencies, constitutional rights can be suspended and marshal law can be declared, e.g., by

FEMA (Federal Emergency Management Authority). The United States was established as a republic in opposition to the British monarchy. Today Great Britain where royalty is purely symbolic is more of a republic that the United States. We have a presidential system of government. Our president is not a symbolic figure but the commander-in-chief whereas in Britain the Queen just accepts people's expressions of homage and accolades. The British Queen does not rule. This is done by the Prime-Minister and his cabinet. Here in the United States the president has the power to issue executive orders without asking Congress. That is the difference.

Sliding to Oligarchy

We have the institution of public opinion that is supposed to control the government or at least restrain it. However, letters, emails and phone calls to congressmen from the electorate are disorganized and are not aggregated into any coherent picture of public opinion. The writers and callers are predominantly from the educated status group; people who can write, who can articulate their thoughts. Yet without the balancing effect of continuous public participation between elections, representative democracy has a tendency to slide into oligarchy, i.e. government of a few. This principle was formulated as an iron law by German sociologist Robert Michels in 1911. While politics is mainly about economic and social policies, our elected officials' primary interest appears to be getting re-elected, not fulfilling election promises. There is a widely spread perception about oligarchy that it is a cabal of a few men sitting together in a smoke-filled room, or else it is a think-tank like the Council of Foreign Relations who make decisions behind our elected government.

At least two political scientists disagree with this view. They write on this point: "Oligarchy can exist with respect to certain limited but crucial policy issues at the same time that many other important issues are governed through pluralistic competition or even populistic democracy. [...] In the US context, as elsewhere, the central question is whether and how the wealthiest citizens deploy unique and concentrated power resources to defend their unique minority interests. In the United States as elsewhere, to the extent that such minority power is exercised, the political system can be considered an oligarchy." The authors present data on income-based material power indices in support of their argument. [1]

After they are elected or re-elected, nothing stops congressmen from forgetting about their campaign promises. Big Media make sure that people's memory-span is as short as the next 30-second commercial. For that reason alone, it is not likely that anyone would remember those promises anyway – let alone demand that incumbents deliver upon them.

If you just write letters to your congressman or call him, they will answer you, they will be polite, they will log your name and address, and that will be the end of it. What they will do with your letters or calls we don't know. Congressmen listen more closely to the checks that lobbyists bring them. The checks are accompanied with requests to give more attention and more legislative benefits to their industry or to their corporation. You can say that it is the lobbyists who are the real representatives in the Congress rather than Congressmen who are in fact lobbyists' spokesmen. Congressmen find it easy to forget their election campaign promises, but they do not forget the interests that bring them checks to fund their re-election. Only participatory democracy equipped with good survey data analysis can control Congress and congressmen's behavior.

We do have democracy but only for very brief periods of election campaigns when politicians need our votes. After we elect them they forget about us – if you don't count the lip service in their speeches and photo opportunities. There is a multitude of organizations working for democracy, but they understand democracy mostly as supporting the ideology of the Democratic Party. They want more equality. They reduce the ideal of social justice to that of equality and entitlements ignoring claim-right and desert as its other important aspects. This is a vey primitive way of understanding social justice as well as democracy. Democracy is government of the people, by the people and for the people, as Abraham Lincoln said.

Yet we try to export our imperfect democracy. So far this only worked well in post-World War II Germany. We tried to export our Western democracy to Iraq and Afghanistan. But it does not seem to work there. A few Western-educated people in those countries try to copy Western institutions such as elections and the parliament. But these institutions remain empty shells as they are devoid of Western values of human rights, and especially the right of free speech upon which public opinion is based.

What happens between elections in our system of government? This is when our democracy is mostly asleep. In fact, participation in rallies and protests, calling, emailing and writing to congressmen is also like voting. In a narrower sense, participatory democracy means continuous, ongoing and organized activity by citizens that would supplement and counterbalance elections. We have elections whose results represent upper class interests. We also have the tradition and the institution of public opinion. But our public opinion is disorganized and toothless. It cannot make Congress listen to it and act accordingly. What is needed is an orderly and institutionalized mechanism that would allow ordinary people to participate more directly in governing our country.

Notes

[1] Winters and Page (2009, pp. 731-732).

2. Democratic Participation by Survey

Abraham Lincoln spoke about government of the people, by the people, and for the people in his Gettysburg address. "Of the people" and "by the people" mean that the government should be elected. "For the people" means that after it is elected, the government is supposed to represent people's will. The reality is that our career politicians are professionals who brag, like any other professional, of their "experience." That is in spite of Jefferson's warning against presidents becoming kings. Politicians vie for power both as members of political parties and as individuals against members of their own party. They do so by skillfully manipulating voters' minds with convenient and demagogical messages through their controlled media of mass communication. Their messages contain good promises that are rarely if ever kept. Their primary goal is not the common good, but rather acquiring power and holding on to it. But power always corrupts. The very idea of power is contrary to the idea of democracy.

The United States is a model society for representative democracy. However, without the complement of popular participation, our representative democracy can easily degenerate into oligarchy or the aristocracy of a select few wealthy families. These families have the money to run or to fund election campaigns. What Lincoln implied in his idea of government for the people was a two-way relationship between the government and the people. This is the idea of participatory democracy. Participatory democracy is about citizen's direct participation in government – especially between elections and in addition to voting. This is also what de Tocqueville must have meant when he wrote about civic associations as based on "self-interest rightly understood."

For Participatory Democracy

We often complain about our Government blaming it for all kinds of failings. Yet we refrain from taking part in governing our own country except by periodically giving the elite license to do that - even when we know that they will not or cannot deliver on their campaign promises. Reconciling election results with public opinion aggregated with rational tools of social science is such a mechanism that will complement electoral representation. Our Constitution gives Congress too much weight compared to the potential weight of public opinion. But even with its limitations our system of representative democracy must be considered a great achievement. Our public opinion cannot force Congress to do anything. When we contact our congressmen, we just blow off our steam but mostly achieve nothing.

The United States is a model society and the leading world power. Today we have the American Empire that acts as a world policeman. As part of this role in the world, our government collects and keeps information on everybody. We can send troops anywhere in the world, topple foreign governments, and install new political regimes that are friendlier to us. All this is all done in the name of democracy and human rights. And yet our liberal-representative democracy is not sufficient for good government.

In his speech Lincoln implied that the democratic idea was a two-way relationship between the people and the government. This is the idea of participatory democracy. Participatory democracy is about citizen's direct participation in government – especially between elections and in addition to them. Participation in rallies and protests, calling and writing to congressmen is also like voting. As opposed to direct democracy, participatory democracy means public participation in the sense of complementing elections and the whole idea of representative democracy. It means counterbalancing the institution of elections with continuous, ongoing activity by organized citizens.

Checks and balances can exist not only among the branches of Government but also between Government policies and public opinion. Participatory democracy means interactive government. There is congressional oversight of executive and intelligence branch activities. There are also public watchdog organizations and whistleblowers. They are insufficient and/or ineffective. One reason is that our election campaigns are as a rule professionally staged and scripted. On the other hand, we are distracted from taking part in governing our country by sensationalized news stories and by stupefying commercial messages.

For public opinion to have an effect on public policies, it must be as good as decisions made in Congress by elected government officials. This can be done by using the power of public opinion. One reason for not doing that is that we are distracted from taking part in governing our country by sensationalized petty news stories, by low-quality popular entertainment, and by commercials for goods that we do not need.

The idea of participatory democracy presumes both liberty-rights and election of representatives but does not stop there. It uses these forms of government to achieve broad social participation and social harmony. Participatory democracy has been tried in the Soviet Union instead of representative democracy,[1] and it failed.

Most advocates of participatory democracy, including Carole Pateman of 1970 and Sidney Verba conceive of participatory democracy as replacing representative.[2] Replacing representative democracy with participatory democracy is a sheer utopia. This would be detrimental to the whole idea of democracy as the Russian experience showed. Participatory democracy was practiced in Soviet Russia at the very beginning of its revolution, in 1918-1919. But then its national Assembly (*Uchreditelnoe sobraniye*) was disbanded by the Bolsheviks and a regime of proletarian dictatorship was instituted, a totalitarian system of government whose results are well known today. Participatory democracy can only be complementary to representative democracy. Democracy needs elections. Given the size and the complexity of our advanced social system it is impossible to do without them.

Interactive Government

To be effective, the system of checks and balances between elected officials and public opinion must be institutionalized in the form of a constitutional amendment. If this is done, it will be a continuation of the historic trend of complementing government run by elites with popular representation that started in the English parliament when the House of Commons was added to the House of Lords. For public opinion to have an effect on public policies, it is necessary to demonstrate that it can be as good as decisions made in smoke-filled rooms by elected government officials and civil service experts. We can demonstrate with social science tools how this is possible.

Participatory democracy as it is conceived here does not reject representative democracy, it is rather meant to complement it. If you want to express your own ideas in government you need to get elected. You can express your own political ideas in Congress or in your local government. We are talking here about the division of labor between representation and participation.

Surveys provide an effective tool for participatory democracy. They have some unique advantages. They require no initiative on the part of the otherwise busy and uninterested public, and no material resources. As Sidney Verba wrote, "Surveys are especially useful for dealing with issues of democratic representation. Participation is a mechanism for representation, a means by which governing officials are informed of the preferences and needs of the public and are induced to respond to those preferences and needs. It is crucial, therefore, to know how well or how badly the participatory system represents the public to those leaders. But how do we know what the 'real' picture is, the interests, preferences, and needs of the public? The sample survey is key to answering this question".[3]

Like any other form of public opinion, surveys can be misused and abused, and the rate of non-response to polls is growing, now between 25 and 30 percent. With all its known weaknesses, surveys can be a powerful tool of political participation. Properly conceived and executed, surveys can become a major tool of participatory democracy. A survey can become such a mechanism if its results and recommendations are taken as complementary to legislation passed by Congress. By setting agendas and addressing issues similar to those in Congressional committees, survey results could then compete with debates in Congress or state legislative bodies on an even and competitive footing.

Surveys could address issues that do not find their way to the floor of the Congress for one reason or another. This would also discipline congressmen and make them work harder and more conscientiously in the public interest. A division of legislative labor could also take place between surveys and the Congress, and thus between representative and participatory democracy. Congress could be responsible primarily for macro-social (economic) issues while surveys primarily are for micro-social ones.

The will of the people will find its expression in an organized way – rather than being manipulated by corporate-owned mass media or in frustrated demonstrations of the Occupy Wall Street type. This will also sharpen and streamline the work of social scientists in developing procedures and methods of better combining the macro and the micro-social worlds and adapting them to each other.

Participatory Forms of Government

The United States was established as a democratic republic in opposition to British monarchy. The same happened in France and in other European nations. Thomas Jefferson envisioned popular or participatory democracy as supplementing the idea of representative democracy that was promoted by Madison. Participatory democracy can energize and empower the people. This is what the French traveler de Tocqueville saw in the young United States in the 1830's. He wrote about "the irresistible and universal spread of democracy throughout the world."[4]

Participatory democracy can bring vitality and vigor to all those politically apathetic couch potatoes who are losing trust in our virtually one-party system of government at an increasing rate. Lincoln's slogan "government of the people, by the people, and for the people" can then acquire an actionable meaning, and not just an aphorism or a catchy rhetorical line. This is how ordinary people can help make policy decisions. Such decisions can be no less valid than the decisions made by elected government using civil service experts.

Since Montesquieu we have been taught that in a democratic government political power is divided into three branches with certain checks and balances among them. In reality there are four such branches rather than three. In addition to the visible legislative, executive, and judicial branches all Western governments also have an invisible informative branch. The informative branch of US government consists of what is called "the intelligence community." This is a ghost of secretive organizations known mostly by their acronyms: NSA, CIA, FBI, the Secret service, DHS. For example, the NSA - National Security Agency - prefers to say that its acronym means "No such agency."[5] Montesquieu overlooked the secret police that has always existed in all countries of the world. The idealistic framers of the American Constitution followed Montesquieu in the regard. We need to acknowledge this fourth branch of government and include it in the system of checks and balances.

Here are some elements of participatory democracy in branches of US government. Taking surveys, answering survey questions and survey data collection serve as the participatory form of informative branch. Here also belong the press, journalism, especially investigative reporting and blogging in the internet. Survey data analysis with policy recommendations serve as the participatory form of the legislative branch. Political activism, neighborhood watch and such serve as participation in the executive branch. Trial by jury and provision of public defenders are participatory forms of the judicial brunch power.

Participatory Democracy is Possible

Democracy is hollow if it is only about the form of government. The substantive meaning of democracy and its purpose is social progress, or progressive social development. This is also the meaning we can attribute to macro-social, economic public policies aiming to improve current social structures that fall short of social progress or upward social mobility.

Some people say ours is a just society, others say it is not. Apparently, both are right since one can look at a partially filled glass also as a partially empty one. So how fair are American social structures? Social scientists have known since the 19th century that everyday social problems are but symptoms of a relatively unjust social system. Raise the level of social justice and you have substantially contributed to the solution of numerous social problems. Social justice is an ideal that we aspire to. It is one of the central demands of American public opinion. The entire human civilization and all its societies can be said to exist and operate owing to better or worse realizations of this idea.

Public opinion exists in a multitude of forms – as rallies, town meetings and demonstrations, the press and the Internet. Its sharpest and the most scientific form is the random and representative survey. Surveys are a tool to aggregate public opinion in the form of responses to questions. When survey results are properly analyzed they can become a powerful tool of direct public participation in government.

Surveys are done everywhere but for other, instrumental reasons, not as an integral part of government. Analysis of survey data will demonstrate how it can serve as a tool of participatory democracy. Such an analysis is not an end in itself. It is but a tool of participatory democracy. We cannot simply trust our elected government to do it for us. We have to make the government work hard for us by showing that we the people also have a tool for governing the country, and not just the Congress with its numerous committees. We the people in the spirit of Lincoln's idea of the government for the people also have a tool for setting public policies. The least it can do is to discipline the elected government. Elected officials will do their work better if they know that someone understands their business, that someone is watching them. That is the idea.

Notes

[1] The word Soviet means council in Russian.
[2] See Pateman (1970, 2012); Verba (2003) also seems to have thought of survey democracy as replacing representative. But then he had second thoughts about its possibility.
[3] Verba (1996, p.1).
[4] de Tocqueville (1988, p. xiii).
[5] Some claim that our intelligence services are just the enforcement arm of the oil and banking industries (Gonzalez, 2010).

3. Aspiration to Social and Cultural Mobility

The question that we face as a community and society is this: How successful are we in our efforts to change our social conditions for the better? According to the founding fathers all men are created equal. They may have meant natural rights, but in today's world the expression, "All men are created equal," could not be further from the truth. Every new generation finds that we are all unequal. We all know since childhood that there are rich and poor people, educated and uneducated people, manual and service (or white-collar and blue-collar) workers. This social condition is called social stratification, a term borrowed from geology and archaeology. Social stratification includes two kinds of layered inequalities: status groups or strata and classes.

We are used to speak of society as consisting of sovereign individuals. This is no different from thinking of the physical world as consisting of atoms of matter. In this perspective, society is viewed as a mass of such atomized individuals with wise benevolent rulers or leaders forming this mass into a shape that they want just like housewife forms bread from dough. Perhaps this was a proper way to imagine social relations 200 years ago, but not today. In today's typical situations there are no individuals, nor is there society as a mass of atomized individuals. Situations such as depicted by the Marlboro man cowboy image, or Clint Eastwood characters, or Robinson Crusoe are possible in reality. But they must be considered quite rare.

Instead of an amorphous mass of atomized individuals we must speak of structures of status groups and classes that are socially stratified. We all belong to a status group or stratum and to a social class. Knowing this is not different from knowing that we speak in prose. Moreover, since we all move across multiple social institutions, we belong to several institutional types of status groups and to multiple social classes at the same time. Think of family status, of educational status, or of occupational status. Think of financial class, employment class, or management class. We can be higher in one type of status and lower in another, higher in one type of social class and lower in another.

Social Stratification

Participatory democracy requires identification of these constructed collective identities rather than primordial ones such as those defined by race and gender. Constructed social identities are groups of stratified social status (high, low, and medium) and stratified social class (upper, lower, and middle). Public opinion polls are funded by and taken primarily in the interest of the elites that form our Government, i.e. high status groups and upper classes. They use the categories of race, sex, ethnicity, and religion that divide rather than unite the general public. The mere use of these categories in opinion surveys and in public discourse promotes sexism and racism. The best way to fight gender and racial discrimination is to drop these categories from social discourse altogether and be color-blind and gender-blind.

As an alternative of corporate power, its critics propose defense of the family, children, the poor, and the powerless. These are exactly what we call status groups. We can speak of family, educational, income and occupational status groups. We all belong to certain status groups and to certain social classes. Eliminating class interests and their representation by elections is a utopian idea leading to anarchy and the rise of extremist political forces. This is what happened in 20th-century Europe when totalitarian dictatorships replaced democracies. In the case of Soviet Union it was fledgling participatory democracy that was replaced by totalitarian communism.[1]

This structural approach helps to analyze relations among all status groups and classes in an unbiased way. We can begin developing this approach by taking a closer look at these two realms of social reality that are usually maladjusted to one another. A good way to start is to discuss units of social relations, their institutions and procedures that can be applied to their structures.

Presenting social structures in absolute terms will not be helpful. It is more helpful to think of social structures in relative terms, in terms of the relative positions which status groups and classes occupy in the structures of social stratification. It is useful to analyze survey results in terms of proportions of people populating unequal social classes and status groups or strata. Status groups belong to the micro-social world, classes to the macro-social.

Ascribed and Achieved Social Status

There are two kinds of social status and status groups: ascribed and achieved. Examples of ascribed social status are race, gender, ethnicity and religion. Ascribed status groups are real. We are born into them. We cannot easily change our ascribed social status. The use of categories of ascribed social status in public discourse, in pubic policies and in government is superficial and provides bases for discrimination. Fighting racial, gender and other kinds of discrimination is divisive and based on victim mentality. It tends to exaggerate grievances rather than resolve them. It is therefore self-defeating. What people in all groups of ascribed social status want is achievement and fairness in the distribution of social benefits, such as education, occupational prestige, higher earnings and organizational promotion. It is these types of benefits that define the main institutional types of achieved social status – educational, occupational, income and family status.

Attaining higher levels of achieved social status is much more important to most people than promoting their special identities as blacks or whites and as women or men. Every structure of achieved social status consists of a number of related elements that are arranged in a hierarchy

– high, low, medium-high and medium-low. The number of members in these groups of stratified social status is usually not the same. Thus social status is distributed among the membership of status groups, and that is where questions are raised about distributive social justice. It is believed that we humans have a built-in sense of justice. Social injustice erodes the fabric of any society. It erodes our social bonds. In extreme cases, this can result in total social disintegration. Public policies, and policies geared to distributive social justice in particular, are based on the idea of directing the processes of social mobility in the upward direction, i.e. of increasing the relative proportion of higher status groups at the expense of lower ones.

Race categories may be appropriate in medical practice to identify people prone to certain diseases such as sickle cell anemia, but not in matters of distributive social justice. The use of gender categories may be appropriate in public bathrooms, but not in matters of social justice. What people in all groups of ascribed social status want is achievement and fairness in the social distribution of education, occupational prestige, higher earnings, and organizational promotion. These are the main types of achieved social status - achieved educational status; achieved occupational status; achieved income status and achieved family status.

Every social structure consists of a number of related elements - groups of different social status: high, low, medium-high and medium-low. This is what is called social stratification, and this is where questions are raised about distributive social justice. We can be higher in one type of status group and lower in another, higher in one type of social class and lower in another. Social mobility means changes in the structural relations among status groups or classes as a result of people moving among them. These movements may be from lower groups to upper ones and from upper to lower ones. Accordingly we speak of upward and of lower social mobility. Pitirim Sorokin who pioneered the concept of social mobility also observed changes in the structural relations among groups of cultural orientation such as different social beliefs and desires.[2] In these cases we can also speak of cultural mobility.

Social Mobility

We tend to find something wrong with the existing structure of social inequalities into which we are born, and we try to improve our position in it. Distributive social justice is about who gets what, what slice of our American pie, and whether the resulting distribution is fair or unfair whether in education, occupational prestige, or position in a formal organization. A social structure improves when the proportion of lower status groups and lower social classes is reduced relative to the proportion of higher ones. The same idea is expressed in increasing the proportion of higher status groups and classes relative to lower ones. Both statements are based on the relational view that all status groups and all classes in a social structure add up to 100 percent. The quantitative differences among social structures are relational — the differences between proportions of higher and lower groups or classes.[3]

In popular opinion, distributive social justice is often equated with the principle of equality meaning an equal distribution of social benefits. The notion of social equality has two different meanings that must be distinguished and not confused. One meaning of social equality is social acceptance or social inclusion, i.e. inclusion without discrimination. In recent history this involved primarily equal rights for African Americans and women. The second meaning of social equality is equality as a principle of social justice in the distributive sense.

The principle of distributive equality is often confused with the idea of equal inclusion, or equality before the law without regard for race, ethnicity, age, gender and today also of sexual orientation. Distributive social justice is a relative concept. The question is always: fair relative to whom? Those who demand distributive social equality always want to be equal to status groups that are higher than their own, not to lower ones. And they want someone else to arrange it for them, for example, by the government without spending much effort of their own. If this is a demand for upward social mobility, maybe this is not the best way of achieving it.

Demands for social equality as the only principle of social justice are often fed by the illusion of eliminating poverty that is promoted by demagogical politicians. Poverty is not an absolute but a relative concept. It is always based on comparisons to higher status groups. In this sense poverty and social stratification in general has always existed and will always exist. The idea is not to eliminate it but to reduce its levels. Equality is only one aspect of distributive social justice, and not even the most important one.

The principle of social equality owes its popularity to the legacy of the 20th century, to the continuing influence of socialist ideas despite the collapse of communist political regimes. Its roots are in the classic utopian socialism of Robert Owen, Charles Fourier, and Saint Simon. Utopian socialism has been practiced in the USSR, China, Cuba, and North Korea without much success. As an alternative, the idea of equality of opportunity has been proposed which boils down to lack of discrimination and equal inclusion. Equating social justice with equality is problematic because the idea of social justice is much broader than equality.

The subject-matter of social justice is more complicated. There are other principles of fair social distribution that are at least as important if not more. Social justice also includes the principles of desert, of claim-right, and of entitlement. Distributive social equality is only one of its principles. Even though it is imposed by the ideological norms of political correctness, the demand for distributive social equality as the sole principle of social justice is utopia, a complete impossibility.

Social Mobility Research

There are two themes invariably recurring in reviews of social mobility research. One is that it is mostly confined to shifts in occupational status, and the other, that fifty years of social mobility research has produced negligible results. The only tangible advances have been in data collection and statistical techniques of data analysis. Not only have the results been poor in terms of answering the original social mobility questions posed by Sorokin, but the range of those questions has been narrowed considerably. S. M. Miller, a prominent figure in first-generation, post-World War II mobility research, wrote, "Despite the diversity of interests, mobility has been studied in a limited and traditional way. Namely, that mobility involves a major change up or down in an individual's occupational position. [...] This emphasis neglects other dimensions of mobility: movements in economic and/or political power; movements in social position in community. While occupational change correlates to an extent with changes in income, social position and political power, it is not a reliable indicator of such change".[4]

Twelve years later and four years after the publication of Blau and Duncan's acclaimed *American Occupational Structure*, it was stated bluntly: "Unsolved problems of stratification theory and research have become chronic diseases of the analysis and interpretation of mobility studies and have limited the theoretical relevance of their results."[5] Still more recent reviewers conceded that "with respect to problem development and theory formulation the field has become excessively narrow," and that it "is evident that firmly established conclusions regarding societal variations and similarities in the structure and process or intergenerational social mobility are not numerous."[6] A better approach is necessary.

Social mobility is the language of the calculus, or the currency in such social exchange that is evaluated in terms of improved or worsened lifestyles and higher or lower social statuses. While in concrete acts of exchange it is sufficient to have the meeting of the minds, the fairness of generalized social exchange depends on the (narrower or broader) extent of social relations. On the societal scale and increasingly so with the progress of globalization the fairness in social exchange is judged by standards of distributive justice that serve as abstract quantitative representations of social stratification. While scales of such quantitative values are not to be found anywhere in the empirical world, their existence materializes in statistical sampling distributions. The appropriateness of specific statistical models of distributive justice holds to the extent that such models are meaningful not only within general-logical and mathematical-probability theories but also as concrete representations of societal ideals of fair social distribution. Accepted models of just social distributions become mathematical-statistical specifications for vague, verbally described standards of distributive justice.

Given the freedom of collective behavior and social exchange, this circulation social mobility of individuals among categories of social structure is a private matter, be it in choosing a marriage partner, a career, or a government. By contrast, its outcomes, i.e. change in the size of the categories of structural social mobility, is a matter of public scrutiny and social control. As structural mobility falls short of standards of distributive social justice, it creates social structural tensions.

Ideal Types and Indicators

In their research work sociologists confront the sharp difference between lofty meanings of abstract general concepts and the unique meanings of lived human experience captured in raw survey data. They bridge this precipice by constructing particular meanings having correspondences in both sets - in abstract general sociological categories and in the unique local meanings of lived social reality.

This mediation between observational data and abstract conceptual schemes is made possible by social indicators and ideal types. Social indicators and ideal types carry and reconcile the two seemingly irreconcilable aspects of their origin. In their inductive empirical aspect, social indicators supply substantive meanings to the abstract notions such as social justice, social structure, social change, and social development. In their deductive modality, ideal types can produce new domain-specific concepts that have a foundation in general theory and methodology. They can then be used as formal building blocks for social sciences. Ultimately, only a solid system of social - or perhaps they should better be called sociological - indicators and ideal types built around major categories of social differentiation can give social research comprehensiveness and cumulative discipline.

Social indicators and ideal types are uniquely positioned to provide a systematic set of middle-range sociological categories that are meaningful both in terms of common-sense observational variables that are part of everyday language, and in terms of the abstract and esoteric language of general sociological theory. Once their operational definitions are constructed and deployed within a consistent scheme of social differentiation, social indicators and ideal types can be used critically to evaluate quantitative relations among a great variety of social groups. The resulting picture of social relations can form the deep structures of synchronic as well as diachronic social change.[7] To be sure, any representation of social structures is in some sense inadequate. First of all, it is usually outdated, referring to a more or less distant past. Secondly, what it tells us about our social world is but a snapshot of innumerable intertwined processes of social change.

To cover available survey data systematically and comprehensively, we must first identify their ideal types and empirical indicators. Selection of indicators requires a differentiation of raw survey data. To be systematic and comprehensive we differentiate survey variables into status groups and classes and further on into their specific institutional domains. In terms of institutional domains for status groups we can speak of family, income, educational and occupational distributive justice. As for institutional domains of economic class relations, we can isolate environmental, financial, employment and management class structures. Still further social differentiation of survey variables involves their social stratification. It is useful to limit the number of categories of social stratification to four and speak of high, low, medium-high and medium-low status groups and upper, lower, upper-middle and lower-middle classes.

In terms of direction, deviations of social stratification from fair social distribution can be positive or negative. In terms of amplitude, they can be tolerable or excessive. The line separating excessive and tolerable departures of social stratification from ideals of distributive social justice is not static. The more deviations from distributive social justice are considered acceptable and are tolerated, and the fewer of them are considered as excessive and intolerable, the larger the sections of society that are unfairly disadvantaged and unfairly privileged. Such deviations cut across the disparities existing between upper and lower strata. Positive deviations from distributive justice involve a relative surplus of values in some social strata and their relative deficit in some others which means that such social strata are unfairly privileged in social mobility, be it in terms of power, wealth, knowledge, or happiness. A negative deviation signifies a deficit of values in a social stratum and an unfair disadvantage in social mobility. Upper strata can have unfair advantages and unfair disadvantages just as lower or middle ones as is evident from the current welfare and affirmative action controversies.

Notes

[1] See Pateman (1976).
[2] Sorokin (1949, 1957). Sorokin avoided using the term social classes speaking instead of economic, political and occupational strata.
[3] As Brown (1976, p. 334) put it, "Rather than expunge normative elements and arguments from research in order to

avoid arbitrariness, one must include them both to avoid this charge and to preserve objectivity."

[4] Miller (1975, p. 22).

[5] Mayer and Muller (1975, p. 170; 1981, pp. 479, 481).

[6] These critical evaluations were not made by skeptic and unsympathetic outsiders like Lewis Coser, but by renowned researchers of social mobility themselves. Coser's charge of using a method without theory, bolstered by C. Wright Mills' haunting charge of abstract empiricism, evoked rather defensive denials. This exchange brought to the fore the unclear status of social stratification theory. As it is realized, what passes for such theory is actually a tacit collective acceptance mostly of Blau and Duncan's attempt at "a quasi-deductive theoretical exercise or else [...] speculation which was prompted by, rather than rigorously tested against, empirical data." See Ganzeboom, Treiman, and Ulice (1991, pp. 278, 297); Horan (1978), Featherman (1981); Goldthorpe (1987, p.552).

[7] "The most obvious strategy for coping with complexity is to break problems into ever-smaller sets and subsets, seek resolution in each subcategory, and aggregate an overall solution" (Dryzek, 1989, p. 104).

4. Modeling and Evaluating
Social Status

Survey democracy is a major tool of public participation in government. Based on survey data analysis, it is possible to pass judgment, to what extent certain elements of party platforms are more or less progressive. Now that we have defined the system of categories for survey data analysis – policy goals, their institutional and empirical domains - we can go ahead and do estimates of social conditions' fairness and the rationality of possible ways of achieving them. What we want is to find out how much the United States has advanced in terms of all these abstract concepts. To do that, we must subject these concepts to empirical analysis and evaluation.

This calls for operationalization of abstract sociological concepts. There is always some social distribution and redistribution taking place. The question is how fair it is. Status group structures are products of the processes of status attainment. Structures of social classes are outcomes of the class formation processes in different institutional domains.[1] To find empirical indicators of status and class structures we aggregate relevant survey data into four stratified groups from high to low. Such indicators will be further differentiated by their institutional domains. Once we have reduced general abstract concepts to their ideal types and raw survey data to their empirical indicators, we can use them to compare and evaluate various social structures with a view of determining social policies as expressions of people's continuous participation in government.

Modeling Social Structures

In social science we operate with models. The alternative would be endless arguments and arbitrary decisions by bureaucrats. The idea of social justice may appear somewhat complicated, and its principles may sound somewhat fuzz. We try to simplify the reasoning behind it to make policy decisions more transparent. This is what is achieved by the use of mathematical models whose properties are known and which allow us to conduct measurements and evaluations in a controlled way.[2]

An evaluation of social conditions can be accomplished with the help of a model of four-parameter standard normal distribution and the method of multinomial ordinal probit analysis that is based on that model. In music simultaneous sets of sounds (chords) are considered to be in harmony because differences between and among them belong to a certain ideal order. There must also be such an ideal order of harmonious social relations that can serve as a model for evaluating real social structures.[3] Social harmony is proportionality to such an ideal or to its best approximation. It is also akin to Aristotelian temperance - as avoiding social structural extremes. It is a challenge to translate these metaphors into procedures and techniques of quantitative research of social justice. It can be conceived as a relative growth of higher strata and a reduction of lower ones with the assumption of a constant sum.

Such a model has been proposed using a monotonically increasing and monotonically decreasing unimodal four-parameter standard normal distribution where the difference between any two adjacent points on its curve is infinitesimal. The symmetrical bell curve of normal distribution is very popular in statistical analysis owing to its very convenient properties. For example, the area under the curve always equals one. However, empirical social distributions are never symmetrical, and we must account for their skewed shapes. We can do that by adding skewness to the two parameters of the symmetric bell-curve. Then we can account for both negative and positive skewness on the normal curve. This curve will still be normal as the area under it will still always be one, but it can now have any possible form of skewness, either positive or negative. We know how to measure the skewness of such curves and how to estimate their empirical parameters. Social distributions can also have different peakedness (or kurtosis). Social distributions must also account for this parameter.

The model uses these four parameters of statistical central tendency: mean for location of the distribution on a standard z-scale, standard deviation for its spread, skewness for its shape, and kurtosis for its peakedness. Since we deal with group data we operate with probits of all these four statistics. We find probits as middle values of their group ranges. Its density function is:

$$
\begin{cases}
\dfrac{1-k}{\sigma\sqrt{2\pi}}\, e^{-\frac{1}{2}\left[\frac{z-\mu}{\sigma(1-a)}\right]^2} + \dfrac{1+k}{\sigma\sqrt{2\pi}}\, e^{-\frac{1}{2}\left[\frac{z-\mu}{\sigma(1-a)}\right]^2} & \text{if } \ z-\mu \ge 0 \\[2em]
\dfrac{1-k}{\sigma\sqrt{2\pi}}\, e^{-\frac{1}{2}\left[\frac{z-\mu}{\sigma(1+a)}\right]^2} + \dfrac{1+k}{\sigma\sqrt{2\pi}}\, e^{-\frac{1}{2}\left[\frac{z-\mu}{\sigma(1+a)}\right]^2} & \text{if } \ z-\mu \le 0
\end{cases}
$$

where $a = \tanh(\gamma_1)$; $k = \tanh(\gamma_2)$.

Despite all the limitless variability carried by the four variables, the area under the normal curve will always be one. The mean parameter of standard normal distribution characterizes its location on the standard z-scale that can be anywhere between its extreme values of plus and minus three, approximately. Social distributions can also have wider or narrower spread along this scale. The flatter the curve the wider will be the spread the distribution. The other two parameters – skewness and kurtosis - both carry properties of mean and standard deviation. The skewed shape of a distribution designates both its location on the standard scale and its spread at the same time. Kurtosis also carries qualities of both these simpler statistics, mean and standard deviation. As in standard deviation, kurtic distributions can have thinner or thicker tails and higher or lower peak, i.e. a heavier or lighter center of gravity, as in mean, except that the location is on the vertical rather than the horizontal dimension. Despite all the variability carried by the four variables, the area under the normal curve will always be one.[4]

The differences between structures of the four parameters of empirical social distributions will be treated as deviations. We start with raw survey data. After raw individual data of survey returns are aggregated into groups we see frequencies of categories of sampled population falling into discrete social status groups as they are defined operationally. We then calculate the four parameters of groups' distribution – its mean, standard deviation, skewness and kurtosis. So far these numbers are not comparable at all. But we need to make these two social structures comparable. To do that we transform the four parameters into their unitary forms, i.e. such that are measured on a scale from zero to one. Once social structures are measured on the same scale, they become comparable. The transformation to a unitary scale of measurement is achieved with the help of hyperbolic functions in the following way:

Mean (0,1)
$$M = \frac{1+\tanh(\mu)}{2}$$

Std. deviation (0,1) $\quad D = \dfrac{1 + \tanh\left[\ln(\sigma)\right]}{2}$

Skewness (0,1) $\quad S = \dfrac{1 - \tanh(\gamma_1)}{2}$

Kurtosis (0,1) $\quad K = \dfrac{1 + \tanh(\gamma_2)}{2}$

Consistent with the concept of upward social mobility, this assumes that larger values of mean, of standard deviation and for kurtosis are better than smaller ones, and that smaller values of skewness are better than larger ones. For mean and skewness this means that we prefer relative growth of higher status groups to that of lower ones. For standard deviation this means that we prefer more equal distributions to more unequal ones. For kurtosis this means that we prefer lower centers of gravity. We will also need a standard of comparison.

Evaluating Social Distributions

Consider the social structure of achieved family status in the United States. The high, medium-high, medium-low and low status groups composing this structure are operationally defined by a cross-tabulation of marital status and the number of children (Table 4-1). To find a standard for evaluating this social structure we calculate unitary parameters for all other family structures since 1981 as well as their sum totals. The structure with the highest sum total of unitary parameters will be our standard of comparison.

Operational Definition of Family Status Groups

Question 1   Are you married, separated, divorced, or widowed?
            (1) never married
            (2) separated/divorced/widowed
            (3) married
Question 2   How many children have you ever had?
            (1) none
            (2) one or two
            (3) three or more

		Question 1		
		(1) none	(2) 1-2	(3) 3 +
Question 2	(1) never married	Lw	MH	Hi
	(2) separated/divorced	Lw	MH	Hi
	(3) married	ML	MH	Hi

Table 4-1. Operational definition of family status groups

We find this standard in the data for years 2001-2004 during Bush-43 presidency. Comparing the two social structures we find small excessive deviation mainly in the mean (0.21%) and in the kurtosis (-0.18%) parameters (Table 4-2). But can we say whether even these small changes since the 1980's have been for the better of for the worse? To evaluate the social structure of achieved family status for 2013-2016 we must find a standard of comparison. First we measure the four parameters of the current family structure: 0.551 for mean probit; 1,424 for standard deviation; -0.191 for skewness; and -1.0756 for kurtosis. We then transform these parameters into their unitary forms which give 0.75 for mean; 0.67 for standard deviation; 0.59 for skewness; and 0.90 for kurtosis. These values add up to 2.91.

2013-2016 Structure of Family Status Groups
Compared with 2001-2004

Parameters	43Bush '01-'04		Obama '13-'16		Deviation
Mean	0.76	26.0%	0.75	25.8%	0.21%
Std.deviation	0.67	22.9%	0.67	23.0%	-0.07%
Skewness	0.60	20.5%	0.59	20.4%	0.03%
Kurtosis	0.89	30.6%	0.90	30.8%	-0.18%
Total	2.92	100.0%	2.91	100.0%	0.00%

Table 4-2. Evaluation of family social status

Consider also the structure of achieved educational status groups in the United States. A definite improvement of this social structure can be observed since the 1980's. We define this status distribution operationally in a cross-tabulation of years of schooling and the highest achieved academic degree (Table 4-3). There are higher proportions of highly and fairly educated Americans today, and lower proportions of the uneducated and the undereducated. After calculating unitary values of mean, standard deviation, skewness and kurtosis parameters for these frequencies and their sum we find the standard for evaluation in data for the years of 2009-2012 under President Obama's first term in office. The results of using that social structure as a standard for evaluating current educational social structure are shown as deviations in Table 4-4.

Operational Definition of Educational Status Groups

Question 1 Your highest academic degree?
(1) no high school diploma
(2) HS diploma
(3) junior college, bachelor
(4) graduate degree

Question 2 How many years of education have you
(1) grades 1-9   completed?
(2) grades 10-12
(3) 1-4 yrs of college
(4) 5-8 yrs of college

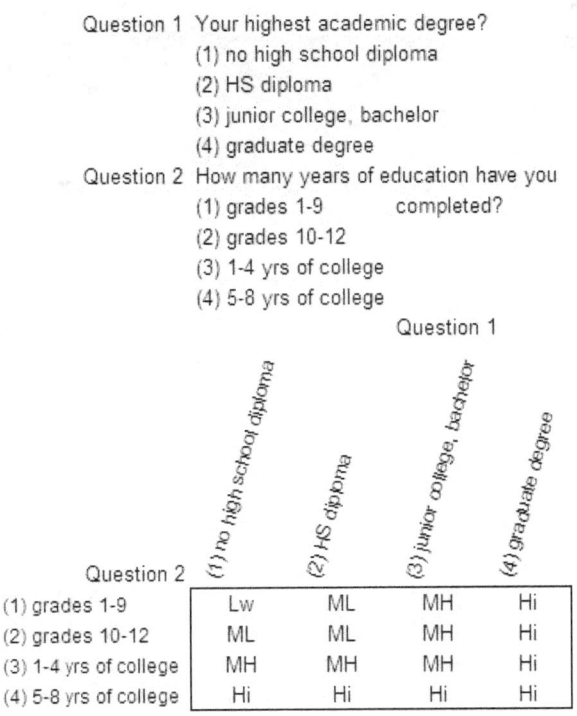

	Question 1			
Question 2	(1) no high school diploma	(2) HS diploma	(3) junior college, bachelor	(4) graduate degree
(1) grades 1-9	Lw	ML	MH	Hi
(2) grades 10-12	ML	ML	MH	Hi
(3) 1-4 yrs of college	MH	MH	MH	Hi
(4) 5-8 yrs of college	Hi	Hi	Hi	Hi

Table 4-3. Operational definition of educational status groups

Let us also consider changes in the social structure of occupational status groups over the past four decades or so. Occupational status groups are defined by occupational prestige where the scores were assigned by survey respondents on a scale from zero to 1. For the purposes of this study the low occupational status was defined as having the low scores up to 37; the lower-middle status as having the scores from 38 to 59; the medium-high as having the scores from 60 to 74; and the high status as having the scores of 75 and higher.

2013-2016 Structure of Educational Status Groups
Compared with 2009-2012

Parameters	Obama '09-'12		Obama '13-'16		Deviation
Mean	0.44	18.8%	0.43	18.7%	2.25%
Std.deviation	0.72	30.8%	0.72	31.0%	-0.94%
Skewness	0.49	21.1%	0.49	21.1%	-0.02%
Kurtosis	0.68	29.2%	0.68	29.3%	-1.30%
Total	2.33	100.0%	2.32	100.0%	0.00%

Table 4-4. Evaluation of educational social status

Looking at a chart of the changes this social structure has undergone since the 1980's, we can see a definite rise in the proportions of all occupational status groups with the exception of the medium-low one that has experienced a sharp decline over the last decade (Figure 1). The 2013-2016 structure of achieved occupational status has the highest sum total of its unitary parameters since the 1980's. For that reason it is also the standard of evaluation. And yet from an impartial point of view we must say that all these status groups of occupational activity must have their fair chance, a chance for social justice in public policy - for distributive social justice, to be exact.

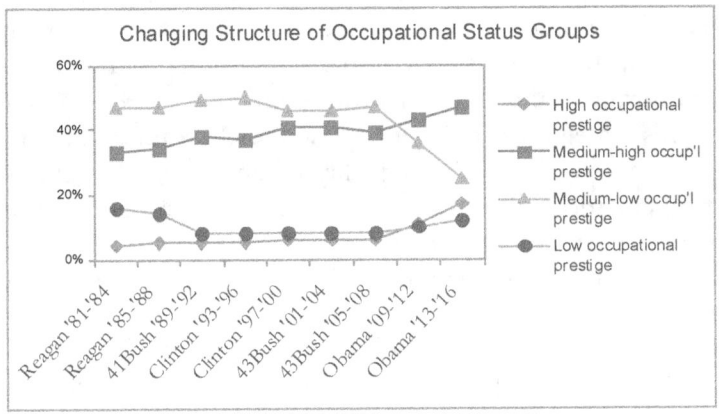

Figure 1. Changing structure of occupational status groups

On Social Differentiation

The content of such policies will be determined by reversal of empirical social structures' excessive deviations from their best exemplars as standards of comparison. This is not much different from medical practice where doctors try to eliminate or reduce excessive deviations of indicators of disease from accepted ideal notions of health. Social policies, too, are aimed at eliminating or reducing excessive deviations of prevailing reality captured in survey data. We speak in this context of distributive social justice, of social consciousness and social conscience.

Sociologists assume that behind all observed social phenomena there is a continuous process of rebuilding social practices that are meaningful to actors and to others who interpret these practices in terms of new and recurring procedures of action.[5] According to Luhmann social differentiation encompasses system segmentation, stratification, and functional differentiation. The meanings of his categories by joining two dichotomies: system-environment and equality-inequality. Functional differentiation in Luhmann is indistinguishable from institutional-structural differentiation. This difficulty can be traced to his understanding of social environment, especially internal.

What appears to be missing here is the equivalent of functional differentiation, namely, institutional.[6] If functional social differentiation, that is an expanded traditional notion of the division of labor, is to be understood as relating to synchronic social functioning then we should also speak of developmental social differentiation. This pair of system categories will then represent a more concrete distinction between social statics and social dynamics (synchrony and diachrony) than the abstract categories of pure structure and process. The success or failure of social movements will strongly depend not only on strategies or pursued collective identities, but also on their correct understanding of the social structures they attempt to change. Ideas about combining micro- and macrosociological perspectives range from their simple juxtaposition[7] to smooth transitions into one another as points on a continuum between the two extremes, but they have not been able to resolve this difficulty.

Notes

[1] Status and class were first differentiated by Weber (1978, pp. 302-307). See Chan and Goldthorpe (2004, 2007) for our contemporary discussion of these concepts.

[2] The notion of mean was introduced in 18th century France by Adolphe Quetlet to designate "average man" (*l'homme moyen*) as a tool for understanding the incidence of marriage, crime and suicide rates. The idea of standard deviation was introduced in England by Francis Galton to the study the unequal spread in the values of height, weight and eyelash length. The skewness statistic that models the shape of a distribution was initially understood as the relationship between centrally located mean and median but then reformulated as the third moment around the mean that can acquire, as mean, negative values in addition to positive ones. Standard deviation being the second moment around the mean is always positive. Finally kurtosis obtains formally as the fourth moment around the mean to designate distribution's peakedness.

[3] Harmony means "fitting together" in Greek. And so it is in any ideal model of social relations.

[4] For more details see Smikun (2011, pp. 146-149).

[5] Cicourel (1973); Bourdieu (1992); Giddens (1984).

[6] Luhmann (1982, pp. 233-237) His definition of functional social differentiation is patently tautological: "*Functional differentiation* organizes communication processes around special functions to be fulfilled at the level of society" (p. 236, emphasis in the original).

[7] Berger and Luckmann (1967).

5. The Ideal of Distributive Social Justice

The idea of social justice is to correct prevailing social structures based on their evaluation. While the ideal of social justice enjoys a universal approval, perceived social injustices generate protests and various forms of social disorganization. The distribution of incomes is one case in point. It is among the most contentious issues in American public opinion. Let us evaluate the American structure of incomes using currently available GSS data for the years 2013-2016. Looking at the chart of changes in the structure income social status since the 1980's we can say that the proportions of the medium-high status group of the "Comfortable" and of the low status group of "Low standard of living" have decreased somewhat.

However, it is not possible to say whether the overall change that includes all four status groups has been for the better or for the worse or how fair it is (Figure 2). A quantitative analysis is in order. Before we try this analysis with a view of drawing policy conclusions from it, we need to consider the principles of distributive social justice as its ideal types and then determine its empirical indicators.

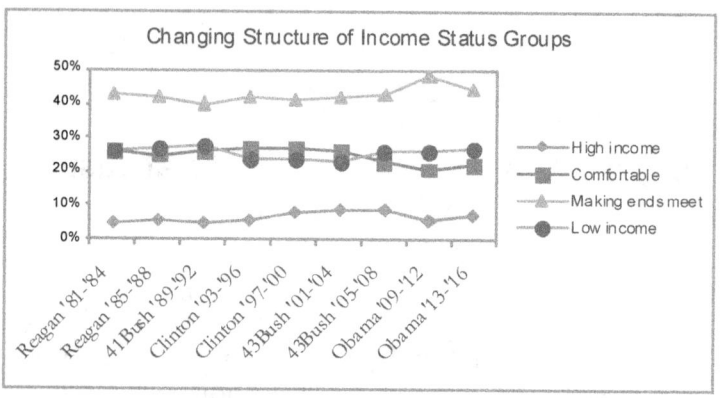

Figure 2. Changing structure of income status groups

Principles of Distributive Social Justice

Next we consider the principles or ideal types of distributive social justice with suggestions for their quantitative modeling. The oldest principle of distributive social justice is Desert - a noun derived from the verb to deserve. Desert is a broader term then merit. Merit usually has a positive meaning. Desert covers both positive and negative territory. According to the principle of Desert, everyone gets or should get what one deserves. The principle of Desert is buttressed by the ideology of individualism and self-interest that supports the profit motive characteristic of laissez-faire capitalism. American individualism is an ideology – deeply rooted in the

American pioneer experience – of brave rugged individuals prevailing over harsh environments.

The next major principle of distributive social justice is distribution by Claim-right. In contrast to the opposite principles of Desert and Equality, Claim-right as the principle of fair social distribution combines the best properties of Equality and Desert as can be seen in class action suits that are brought against entities that are negligent or otherwise cause harm for a class of individuals. Like Equality, both sides in a distributive dispute present their cases in a court of law under the same rules of civil procedure. Like Desert, the dispute is considered on its merits, and the jury of their peers resolves the dispute in an unbiased manner.

Still, despite all its advantages, the principle of Claim-right is not sufficient for distributive social justice. Under this principle, material and non-material benefits become socially distributed in a skewed way favoring some groups and leaving other segments of the population poor and powerless. In the USA, it is believed that there is a very small group of super-rich people and a substantial number of people living in poverty. The use of the principle of Claim-right cannot help to correct this situation by itself. There is one more principle of fair social distribution. After World War II, T.H. Marshall wrote about social rights, or rights of citizenship in addition to political liberties. These were demands that are collected under the name of social citizenship: right to work, to a job providing a living; right to education; right to health care; right to children's welfare.[1]

These conditions are not recognized as rights. They can rather be seen as entitlements. The ideological expression of the distributive principle of Entitlement is social democracy that stresses the outcomes of fair government policies as opposed to their processes. Its practical expressions are found in the Social Security, Medicare and Medicaid programs. Some consider public assistance according to the AFDC welfare program also an entitlement. Welfare programs have both positive and negative aspects. While promoting social justice, welfare programs are tied to inflexible government bureaucracy and can breed a culture of multigenerational dependency. The distributive principle of Entitlement does not curtail freedoms. It only balances them with a provision for social obligations. This is well expressed in John Rawls' philosophy of social justice.[2] His two principles of social justice are: civil liberties accessible to all, and providing for those who are worst off, who are the most disadvantaged.

So which principle of distributive social justice is correct? Just like their ideologies, all the four principles of social justice – Desert, Equality, Right, and Entitlement - are correct and necessary. These four principles of distributive justice operate in the USA - as they can be assumed to operate everywhere else. The question is to what degree. None of these principles is valid if it is elevated as the only true one. Social justice can be found only in a combination of all of them as appropriate to the specific situation. The idea of fair social distribution is more complicated than what we hear in the promises and disputes of political candidates running for elected offices. Not only do they use wrong, divisive categories, but they also ignore the complexities involved in the ideal of distributive social justice. The problem of estimating social justice consists in reconciling these four basic principles – Desert, Equality, Right and Entitlement – and combining them. The question is to what extent and in what proportion.

The ideal of distributive justice sometimes meets with objections against any kind of social redistribution, especially in the lingering fear of socialism. For one thing, redistribution is an integral part and parcel of any government and of American democracy in particular. It finds its expression, for example, in the form of progressive income tax that also provides exemptions for dependents. We Americans pride ourselves for being a fair society in both its economic and democratic senses.[3] What is really behind the objections against social redistribution is the ideal of egalitarian distribution as its only principle, i.e. the idea of command socialist distribution by a central government coupled with prohibition of private enterprise and with denial of democratic freedoms.

The egalitarian socialist command economy of the USSR practiced redistribution by central government ostensibly according to the principle of Equality combined with the ruthless political regime of communist dictatorship. This led to general poverty and eventually to economic and political collapse. Up to 1929 the democratic West also practiced social distribution, but only according to the laissez-faire principle of Desert. This resulted in the disastrous Great Depression that eventually led to World War II in Europe. Today most societies of the world prefer systems of mixed economy that combine multiple principles of social distribution.

Modeling Distributive Justice

Rousseau's idea of original social equality in the uncorrupted state of nature popularized by the French Revolution was cultural in nature. It stood for social acceptance and inclusion of ethnic and religious minorities based on ideals of common humanity and fraternity, or social cohesion. However, when equality is interpreted to mean equal distribution of social benefits among included racial, ethnic, or religious groups, this idea is disputed as a distraction from the deeper social problem of distributive social injustice. The egalitarian ideal has always been on the Romantic and utopian side, and it may still have empirical validity in parts of the world today where famine, disease and poverty are rampant. This is not the case in affluent Western societies where distributive social justice is the predominant idea underlying sustained social relations.

Measuring distributive justice as equality among social strata is the simplest and only partial way. Even more important are degrees of social harmony and social amelioration in various aspects of a stratification system. Social harmony is akin to Aristotelian temperance - as avoiding social structural extremes, or what we call social polarization today. In our time we are not dealing with egalitarian redistribution, but with social justice in its distributive, action sense. As ideal types, the principles of distributive social justice can guide our evaluations of both prevailing social conditions and our actions aimed at improving them. The basis for a critical examination of conditions is provided by their observation. The principles of distributive social justice are Desert, Equality, Claim-right and Entitlement.

We will use the four parameters of central statistical tendency – mean probit, its standard deviation, skewness and kurtosis - to model these principles of distributive social justice. Desert and Equality are the opposites of each other. We find the same in mean and standard deviation that measure the center of gravity and the spread of distributions, respectively. Mean probit of standard normal distribution describes its location of the standard z-scale that can be anywhere between its extreme values of about three, plus and minus. This is similar to the meaning of Desert as the principle of distributive justice that can also be anywhere from the highest to the very lowest social position. Distributions can also have wider or narrower spread along this scale. The flatter and wider the spread of the curve the more Equality is indicated in the distribution.

This is more or less simple. The other two parameters – skewness and kurtosis - are slightly more complicated in their substantive interpretations. They carry properties of both mean and standard deviation. The skewed shape of a distribution indicates its location on the standard scale but also its spread. This is similar to the principle of Claim-right that incorporates both the principles of Desert and of Equality. Indeed, when you have a claim and go to civil court you find that the sides in the dispute are equal before the law. Yet the case is decided on its merits where only one side in the dispute prevails. This is how Equality and Desert manifest themselves in the principle of Claim-right that can be modeled by the skewness parameter of an expanded normal distribution. Entitlement, the fourth principle of distributive social justice also combines certain properties of Desert and Equality except that in our system Entitlement is awarded and administered by government agencies rather than by civil courts.

The distributive principle of Entitlement is also used for upper classes and high status groups, not just for the poor. There does exist corporate welfare, for example, in the form of various tax breaks. Think also of US Congressmen who award themselves huge and still increasing salaries for life. The principle of Entitlement has certain features of Equality or equalizing, but also those of Desert since its recipients must fit certain qualifications. Kurtosis is used to model Entitlement for the similar reason of carrying qualities of these two simpler statistics and principles, mean and standard deviation. As in standard deviation, kurtic distributions can have thinner or thicker tails. As in mean, it can have a higher or lower peak, i.e. a heavier or lighter center of gravity which is an indication of its location - except in the vertical rather than the horizontal dimension. It is on this basis that we can use kurtosis to model Entitlement.

Evaluating Income Distribution

We evaluate social structures by comparing sets of their four statistical parameters in the expanded normal distribution model (Figure 3). The meanings of these parameters closely correlate with principles of distributive social justice.

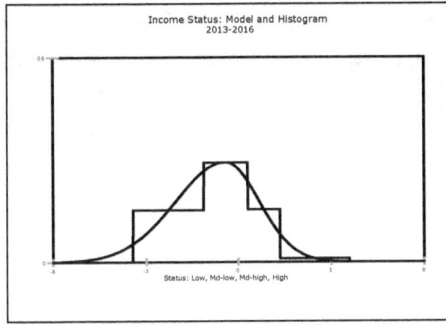

Figure 3. Income status distribution, 2013-2016. Model overlaid on histogram

The indicators of income distribution are operationally defined by cross-tabulating personal income from all sources before taxes in preserving dollars with the direction in which, according to the respondents, their financial standing was changing. Thus the high income status group (Hi) is defined as those having an income over $100000 and whose financial situation has been getting better or stayed the same or else those having an income over $35000 and whose financial situation has been getting better. The low (Lw), medium-low (Ml) and medium-high (Mh) income status groups are defined accordingly (Table 5-1).

Looking at the chart of income status groups from high to low (Figure 2, page 60) we can say that under this operational definition most Americans (about 43%) are just "making ends meet." They fall into the group of medium-low social status followed by the smaller status groups of medium-high and low social status (about 25% each). To have a more precise evaluation of income structure we must look at the parameters of this social distribution. We find a standard for comparing the current income structure in the structure of income status groups for the years 1993-1996 during President Clinton's first term in office. The calculation of unitary parameters from the data on income status shows that their sum total has been the highest for that time period since the 1980's. This qualifies it to serve as a standard of comparison and evaluation. To compare the parameters of these two social structures we first calculate their sum totals as percentages.

Operational Definition of Income Status Groups

Question 1 Personal income from all sources before taxes in preserving dollars
(1) < $10K
(2) $10K-$35K
(3) $35K-$100K
(4) > $100K

Question 2 During the last few years has you financial situation been getting better, worse, or stayed the same?
(1) Getting better
(2) Stayed the same
(3) Getting worse

Question 2

Question 1	(1) < $10K	(2) $10K-$35K	(3) $35K-$100K	(4) > $100K
(1) Getting better	ML	MH	Hi	Hi
(2) Stayed the same	Lw	ML	MH	Hi
(3) Getting worse	Lw	Lw	ML	MH

Table 5-1. Operational definition of income status groups

2013-2016 Structure of Income Status Groups Compared with 1993-1996

Parameters	Clinton '93-'96		Obama '13-'16		Deviation	Tolerated	Excessive	Distributive justice
Mean	0.36	16.4%	0.30	14.3%	2.11%	1.3%	0.8%	Desert
St.deviation	0.66	30.2%	0.65	31.1%	-0.88%	-0.9%		Equality
Skewness	0.44	20.1%	0.41	19.5%	0.57%	0.6%		Claim-right
Kurtosis	0.73	33.3%	0.73	35.1%	-1.80%	-1.3%	-0.5%	Entitlement
Total	2.18	100.0%	2.09	100.0%		absTotal=>	1.3%	
Tolerance						1.34%		

Table 5-2. Evaluation of income social status

When we now compare the two columns of these percentages we find certain deviations of one from the other. These are overall deviations that do not take into account tolerances that we assume exist in our liberal society. What we want to find is excessive deviation, such that go beyond the levels of tolerance. To determine the empirical level of tolerance we can use mean absolute deviation (MAD) as its criterion. Once we know the level of tolerance we subtract it from the values of overall deviations and thus obtain the values of excessive deviations. We find two excessive deviations that go beyond the level of tolerance - a positive deviation of the mean parameter (0.8%) and a negative one for kurtosis (-0.5%).

Having found this value of excessive deviation from the standard of comparison we can now interpret it substantively. American income distribution still relies excessively on the principle of Desert and insufficiently on Entitlement (Table 5-2). The ideal of distributive social justice may appear a bit too complicated, but this is the way to simplify reasoning and make policy decisions more transparent. This is what is achieved by the use of mathematical models that allows us to conduct measurements and evaluations in a controlled way.

Notes

[1] Marshall (1950).
[2] Rawls (1971, 1999).
[3] Schumpeter (1947) was struggling with these ideas.

6. Social Justice for Class Structures

We have demonstrated in some detail a method for evaluating social structures of status achievement. It is necessary to emphasize that the method is more important than the results of this research. Results depend heavily on the quality of data and on the ways we transform them. General Social Survey is considered to be of top quality among all national surveys in the United States. Sill, errors are possible despite the best efforts to avoid them, and this can affect the calculations.

We will now focus on evaluating the fairness of class structures. The ideas of social class and social status group are not clearly distinguished in public consciousness including professional literature. Our imagination is still captivated by concepts of class and social stratification developed by the classics for their particular historic and cultural situations of the 19th and early 20th centuries. The term class was originally used for the zoological classification of animal species. That is the original meaning of class. Only later was it transferred to social groups, initially in France (the nobility, the military and the clergy) and in England (lords, gentlemen and commoners). The difference between social status and class is not always clear. Income status and financial class are often confused as are occupational status groups and management classes. The difference between status and class was well illustrated by President Kennedy when he said in his inauguration speech, "Ask not what the country can do for you. Ask what you can do for your country."

In this sense, what the country can do for you defines the meaning of social status – your family status, educational status, occupational status or income status. Classes are social divisions in the opposite sense, in Kennedy's words, what we contribute to our country such as environmental quality, differences in employment, in management and in financing. Collectively these types of classes define what is called the economy. We will therefore consider all economic relations as relations of social classes.

Wealth of the Nation or of Classes?

We will use the term class in the sense appropriate to our American social and political realities. The two major American political parties were originally formed to represent different class interests. By the time of the Civil War, the Democratic Party represented the wealthy land and slave-owning upper classes of the South. The Republican Party represented the industrial and anti-slavery middle classes of the North. The platforms of these two political parties were switched about the time

Ronald Reagan came to power in 1980 when southern democrats changed their views. Today it is widely believed that the Republican Party primarily represents the interests of the upper classes, and the Democratic Party represents the interests of the lower classes. Likewise it is believed that in Great Britain the Conservative Party represents the interests of the upper classes, and the Labor Party represents the interests of the lower classes.

We can consider the notion of class stratification by comparing the primary concerns of two social sciences: economics and sociology. Since Adam Smith the subject-matter of economics has been understood as ways and means of creating the wealth of a nation. That was the title of his major work that is now a classic. Then Karl Marx insisted that economy is not about the wealth of the nation but rather about the wealth of the upper class, the class of capitalists, and that the wealth of that upper class was created at the expense of the lower class — industrial workers who owned no property, or the proletariat. Marx's perspective was very influential during the 20th century, and it still is in spite of the demise of communist Russia. And so today we continue to associate the platforms of the two major American political parties with interests of different social classes rather than with those of the nation as a whole.

Class divisions and changes in class structures are some of the central subject-matters for the science of sociology. By contrast, economic science is primarily concerned with business and growth. When politicians of both political parties debate in Congress or in election campaigns matters of social and economic policies they freely mix the concepts of these two sciences – economics and sociology. Social justice is one of the strongest popular demands of our time. However, the science of economics is not interested in it despite the fact that social justice is a major factor in raising business confidence and increasing industrial productivity. Shared class interests are related to ongoing changes - for better or for worse – in economic and political life. That is why class structures are seen as consisting of conflicting class interests where we must choose sides – either the side of corporations or the working people. This Marxist view has been followed in Soviet Russia and in their satellite countries in China. And this view failed miserably. The United States has been a strong leader in opposing this view.

Our traditionally flourishing economy is proof of the correctness of USA's opposition to Marxism. Still, the economic science that we use to guide our policies cannot help in resolving the still lingering problems generated by the fiscal crisis of 2008. Government bail-outs after the 2008 financial crisis increased our enormous national debt, but the faulty banking system was left unchanged. Economists continue to advocate the trickle-down theory. Its proponents of this theory say that the bigger the size of the pie, the more resources will trickle-down to the poor without regard for fairness in the distribution of social benefits. For all its primitivism, this theory may be the only attempt to reconcile the perspectives of the two social sciences – of economics and sociology.

After the disaster of the Great Depression, a big discovery was made in economic science: It was found that instead of the fundamental assumption of perfect competition it was more correct to assume that competition in the capitalist marketplace was imperfect, and that seeing private firms as routinely engaging in monopolistic practices was a better representation of empirical reality.[1] And yet, the classic assumption of perfect (or pure) competition is still there in the mainstream neoclassic and post-Keynesian economic theory of today. It remains a solid foundation of all refinements of the basic equilibrium model of matching supply and demand.[2] It is not difficult to agree with Joan Robinson's conclusions and to see, furthermore, that market competition has never actually been perfect in history. As Karl Polanyi noted, the "starkly utopian" self-regulating market system of perfect competition was inconsistent with the international social realities of Europe and North America.[3]

Concerns of the two major American political parties can be reconciled only if we assume the idea of social development which implies both economic growth and distributive social justice. These two ideas do not exclude one another. The aspiration to progressive development or upward class mobility envisages a relative increase of the proportion of people in upper classes with a corresponding relative decrease of their proportion in lower classes. Sociology may have better tools for addressing the problems of social class mobility than the science of economics. However, in many other respects, economics is much more advanced as a science than sociology. We must take time to make sociological sense of certain economic concepts. One such concept is economic inputs as opposed to outputs.

Economists call inputs factors of production. They specify four types of these factors: land, labor, entrepreneurship and capital. These factors are said to be traded in markets as things, as inanimate objects. However, there are people behind all these factors of production and people's social relations. Economists' factors of production stand for different socio-economic institutional domains. The land factor stands for environment, the labor factor for employment, the entrepreneurship factor for management, and the capital factor for financing. This is the human side of economists' factors of production. In the mid-19th century there were antagonistic classes of workers and capitalists as real groups of people. Marx's class analysis may have been valid for his time. However, there are no longer classes of workers and capitalists in the sense Marx used these terms, not in the United States at any rate. Instead today we speak of upper, lower and middle environmental, employment, management and financial socio-economic classes. We often continue to speak of the rich, the comfortable, those just making ends meet, and the poor as stratified classes. But it is more appropriate to speak of them as income status groups.

Employment Class Structure

With this approach, we can see economic policies as based on historic and comparative analysis of class structures. We can use the same evaluation method we use to analyze social mobility in status group structures, i.e. by comparing various class structures and finding their excessive deviations from standards with a view of reversing them as a matter of social policy. In this way, sociological analysis can be fruitfully applied to macro-social, i.e. economic issues and problems. We will start by estimating the fairness of class structures by comparing current ones with the best class structures of the past as standards.

Consider changes in the class structure of employment in the United States. In survey data analysis we make sure that status groups are presented as socially stratified structures. Stratified categories of social classes must be mutually exclusive and exhaustive. This is the principle of any good taxonomy. Employment class structure was measured using respondents' labor force status as its indicator. These raw survey data were then grouped into four large categories: the upper employment class of those working full-time more than 40 hours a week called Work hard; the upper-middle employment class of those working full-time 40 hours a week called Nine-to-fivers; the lower-middle employment class of those working part-time or less than 40 hours full-time called Part-timers; and finally the lower employment class of retired and unemployed called Non-working. By this definition, most Americans belong to the "Work hard" and "Non-working" groups (Figure 4).

To evaluate the current employment structure we must compare it to its best past state. We find such a standard of comparison in the data for the years 1997-2000 during President Clinton's second term that had the highest sum total of parameters since the 1980's.

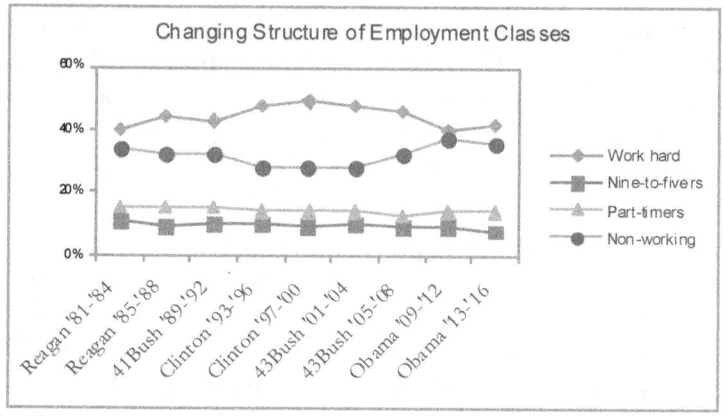

Figure 4. Changing structure of employment classes

This comparison shows that the American employment class structure relies too much on the Desert and too little on the Entitlement principle of distributive social justice (Table 6-1). It appears that Affirmative Action programs still have merits, after all. Entitlement is modeled by the weight of kurtosis tails. Kurtosis has two extremes. Thus the value of kurtosis is relevant to both upper and lower classes of the distribution. There is welfare not only for lower classes but also as tax breaks and other entitlements for the upper classes. In 2008 large financial corporations were considered too big to fail. This is nothing if not entitlement that we as a nation give to financial manipulators enabling them to continue business as usual despite the fact that they caused a major financial crisis on a world scale. This is corporate welfare. The tails of kurtosis and the height of its peak well model this situation.

Financial Class Structure

Looking for a rational basis to improve financial class structure, we compare its current situation to a better earlier one – which happens to be in the years 1993-1996 under President Clinton. This comparison reveals that the popular demands for equality in the distribution of wealth are exaggerated. The object of more concern must be Claim-right and the Entitlement. Our analysis shows excessive deviations in these two principles of distributive social justice: a positive one for Claim-right (there is too much litigation) and a negative one for Entitlement (insufficient attention to deserving classes – be that the rich or the poor or the middle class (Table 6-2).

Financial classes are defined operationally by respondents' evaluation of their families' financial standing cross-tabulated with family income in preserving dollars. We can thus define the upper financial class of the rich (Up), the upper-middle class of the well-to-do (UM), the lower-middle class of those making it (LM), and the lower financial class of the poor (Lo) (Table 6-3). Note the sum of absolute values of excessive deviations marked as absTotal in the tables. These values can be used as an index of distributive injustice. The values of tolerance can be used as an index of social polarization (see Figure 5). Indeed, higher values of tolerance represent just an averaged summary of positive and negative deviations of empirical distributional proportions from the standard.

	Clinton '97-'00		Obama '13-'16		Deviation	Tolerated	Excessive	Distributive justice
Mean	0.89	28.3%	0.63	22.9%	5.4%	4.0%	1.4%	Desert
St.deviation	0.58	18.5%	0.60	21.7%	-3.1%	-3.1%		Equality
Skewness	0.72	22.8%	0.56	20.2%	2.6%	2.6%		Claim-right
Kurtosis	0.95	30.3%	0.97	35.2%	-4.9%	-4.0%	-0.9%	Entitlement
Total	3.13	100.0%	2.75	100.0%	absTotal=>		2.3%	
Tolerance					4.0%			

Table 6-1. 2013-2016 employment class structure compared with 1997-2000

	Clinton '93-'96		Obama '13-'16		Deviation	Tolerated	Excessive	Distributive justice
Mean	0.12	7.4%	0.12	7.2%	0.2%	0.2%		Desert
St.deviation	0.57	33.9%	0.55	34.2%	-0.3%	-0.3%		Equality
Skewness	0.21	12.6%	0.18	11.3%	1.3%	0.8%	0.6%	Claim-right
Kurtosis	0.77	46.0%	0.76	47.3%	-1.2%	-0.8%	-0.5%	Entitlement
Total	1.67	100.0%	1.61	100.0%	absTotal=>		1.0%	
Tolerance					0.8%			

Table 6-2. 2013-2016 financial class structure compared with 1993-1996

Operational Definition of Financial Class Structure

Question 1 Compared to American families, is your family
income above average, average, or below average?
  (1) Above average
  (2) Average
  (3) Below average

Question 2 Family income from all sources in preserving dollars?
  (1) <$15K
  (2) $15K-$50K
  (3) $50K-$150K
  (4) >$150K

	Question 1		
	(1) Above avg	(2) Average	(3) Below avg
Question 2 (1) <$15K	LM	Lo	Lo
(2) $15K-$50K	UM	LM	Lo
(3) $50K-$150K	Up	UM	LM
(4) >$150K	Up	Up	UM

Table 6-3. Operational definition of financial class structure

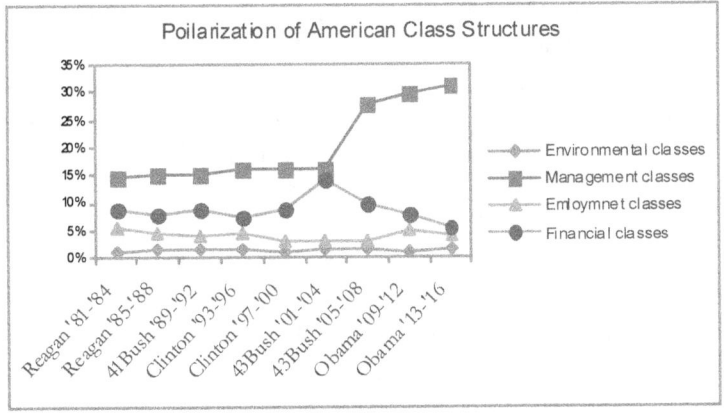

Figure 5. Polarization of American class structures

We have evaluated several different status group and class structures using the statistical model of expanded normal distribution and interpreting its parameters as principles or elements of distributive social justice. The evaluations were done in terms of the best standards we could find in the survey data in the years 1981-2016. Since all these standards were different, the question arises: Is it possible to speak of distributive social justice as something real and not purely relativistic? Is it possible to find a stable guide for public policies aimed at improving social conditions? Is there any truth in such evaluations of prevailing social conditions as a basis for our attempts at improving them?

One answer to this question is that truth cannot be told. Truth is something that we create ourselves by comparing available information and deciding which is more and which is less credible. As children we are taught truths as things, as something objectified. When we grow up we de-objectify (deconstruct) the truths learned in childhood based on our own beliefs. Truth does pre-exist in this sense. Collective truth is created by status group beliefs and class confidence that, in turn, affect collective status group aspirations and class interests.

Notes

[1] Robinson (1933)
[2] Samuelson (1976, pp. 68-70, 632-633)
[3] Polanyi 1944)

7. Rationality in Social Consciousness

Confidence reconciles and harmonizes multiple and contradictory knowledge about the world with the ever-changing situation in which we find ourselves. Social consciousness mediates and reconciles the differences between social conditions and aspirations to upward social mobility. It is the foundation of the stock of knowledge that we use in everyday life as well as in sciences. We can evaluate our social consciousness reflexively against the ideal of rationality. It is useful in this respect to go back to Max Weber and reappraise his distinction between instrumental, goal- and value-rationality that promise more clarity than Haberms' idea of educated elites' polite conversations in a cozy café environment.[1]

The principles and ideal types of instrumental rationality are suggested by the philosophy of cultural sciences since Dilthey and especially Weber. We take them to be facts, meanings, understanding and interpretation. Mere facts do not carry any meaning, nor do the abstract notions of social science, including that of the classics. The reason is that facts are meaningless unless they are properly understood and interpreted. All abstract concepts are sterile unless they are interpreted in terms of what we already know and in what we believe. Instrumental rationality is found in understanding and interpretation based on facts and their meaning.

An understanding of received knowledge about our social world explores it as a collection of social facts, and we treat them as objectified things. In an interpretation we cast facts in a new light using our own ideas and themes that are relevant to today's social concerns. This is a unique and selective process with emphasis laid on some of the facts as against others. This interpretive work is highly reflexive in the sense that we compare actual and possible interpretations of the same facts. We will want to re-interpret their previously understood meanings, and in this way de-subjectify them. Since the number of interpretations of the same social facts is limitless, the criteria for evaluating interpretations must be the completeness of the material covered and the internal consistency of the interpretation itself.

Understanding and Interpretation

Different interpretations do not necessarily negate one another - if for no other reason than because none of the facts are free from ambiguities and contradictions. Preference may also depend on our interpretive interests. We will also want to find valuable commonalities among them. In doing so we may feel free to change the exact meanings behind the facts and to adapt them to today's needs. This will become necessary especially if we then want to present our own ideas.

Interpretation is a narrative that must be internally consistent both with respect to the facts considered and to the interpreter's perspective. It can consist of several layers not necessarily separated in time and in space. So first comes an understanding where we elucidate the central ideas and logic of social facts as well as their possible inconsistencies. One can address certain unresolved problems found in this legacy, such as the relationship between theory and practice in Marx, the problem of positive functions of crime in Durkheim or the problem of value-neutrality in Weber. In such a reading, we should find that some of the central classic concepts - exploitation and class struggle, social values and rationalization, solidarity and social coordination, social integration and exchange - were all rooted substantively or reflexively in problems of social justice and rationality that are also the most fundamental issues of today's social world.

We can then use our gained understanding to de-subjectify the ideas and the senses intended in the social facts by re-interpreting them. In this re-subjectifying work we extract the received ideas out of their historical contexts and use them as material in building our own conceptual schemes still making an effort to do as little violence to their original meanings as possible. We reframe the objectified social facts by combining and re-combining some of their central ideas and categories in an internally consistent conceptual scheme of our own. This must involve above all the concepts of social class, of status group, and of the relationship between them.

Neither the hermeneutic understanding nor the interpretation of facts is an end in itself. Their primary task is to provide a necessary material foundation for a consistent re-conceptualization of conflicting extant usages so that such a re-conceptualization may be grounded and have a chance of being considered valid - if only for a limited time. At this third stage of conceptualization we combine certain ideas and concepts of the considered facts in a single synthesizing conception. In this way we hope to use our understanding to articulate a better concept of and a better method for solving today's social problems. While still trying to preserve as much of their original meaning as possible, we may nevertheless take the received meanings out of their original contexts and adapt them to the problems of today's social concerns as if they all were different aspects of a single new ideal object.

Conceptualization

But is there such a single perspective that will be congruent with inculcated social facts that are usually so different? The answer must be yes since they are all relevant to our efforts in building a valid and useful social consciousness. So the question should rather be how do we find – or construct – such a single perspective? This is equivalent to asking, what relevance do extant ideologies have for us today? Which of their notions and methods are meaningful in today's social realities? There is also a requirement that combining different facts should not be eclectic. Our new conceptual scheme must be internally coherent and consistent. This means is that after de-objectifying received knowledge in the process of its understanding, the work of de-subjectifying interpretation must be based on a synthesizing conceptualization that re-objectifies classic ideas and concepts in a new internally coherent scheme.

Having interpreted facts and having used these interpretations to build our new conceptual schemes, we re-objectify those facts by using them in theory construction and in subsequent empirical testing. This will involve modeling the objects of empirical investigation and thus creating a basis for quantitative empirical research of present-day problems of social justice and rationality. Empirical research will create a basis for constructing a variety of substantive social theories and for their empirical testing that includes modeling and measurement. Quantitatively modeled and measured social structures, social practices, and their underlying social values will make it possible to evaluate past and present social processes and build a better future. We can do all that because our de-objectifying understanding and re-objectifying explanation are mediated by de-subjectifying interpretation and re-subjectifying interpretation.

This picture is complicated by the fact that while any understanding and interpretation needs an ontological frame of reference, in a sense this relationship holds the other way, too. Any ontological presupposition can only be expressed in, justified by, and based upon an understanding and interpretation of meanings that are substantive and concrete in some other, extraneous context. This is what has been described as the hermeneutic circle of understanding. Such a circle can be broken and avoided when the task of semantic understanding and interpretation is separated from the reflexive critique of prevailing misunderstandings and misinterpretations as well as from the critical analysis of pertinent literary material.

The idea of a hermeneutic circle harks back to Hegel's dictum that what is rational is real, i.e. actualized in the historic development of the human Spirit, and what is real is rational. The latter is not necessarily true, however. At any present moment we are faced with multiple realities whose rationality must be questioned. Ontological presuppositions that are always present in our interpretive work are also likely to be polysemantic. Attempts at their explicit interpretation will immediately expose their biases that cannot be rationally justified. Gadamer appropriately called such presuppositions prejudices. But this is just another way of saying that understanding and interpretation mediate between facts and meanings. Conceptualization is also a mediating product standing between de-objectifying understanding and re-objectifying interpretation.

Standards of Rationality

Rationality judgments presume certain normative standards, and such standards are not unproblematic. The promise given by neatly built conceptual schemes successfully to grasp and to interpret empirical social reality never comes without a price. Genuine lived meanings of empirical data are always fuzzy, haphazard, and ultimately unfathomable. While the harmony, comprehensiveness, and consistency imposed by an extraneous conceptual scheme on observed lived meanings may obviate the problem of reliability, the extreme rationality of abstract conceptual meanings may easily rob them of their original validity. Common-sense native meanings cannot be simply replaced with sociological conceptual jargon. The precipice separating them can only be bridged by meanings that are intelligible both in terms of deductively obtained abstract conceptual schemes and in terms of the unique meanings that constitute the language of a local community of natives.

If we have a comprehensive system of such meanings, we can then leap into the less tidy but necessary realm of empirical research. There we will have to readjust our vision to the new perspective. From abstract ideas and concepts such as social process and social structure we will have to come down to the real world of sociological observation and measurement. Reports of indices of social justice and rationality could provide estimates of the levels of justice and injustice in our society with respect to particular facets of its social structures. We can then estimate quantitatively to what degree the social structures of our interest are fair or unfair, rational or irrational.

Adherence to any standards of social justice and rationality cannot by itself guarantee progressive public policies. Social consciousness reflects beliefs of upward social mobility in its pursuit. An evaluation of rationality in social consciousness requires that stratified structural elements of this social value be differentiated with a view of measuring their levels. Policies based on such evaluations can only be put in life provided there is a consensus, an agreement among all status groups or classes involved. Both advantaged and disadvantaged groups must agree to certain redistribution as necessity on the part of members of all such groups. To achieve the ideal of social justice certain means are necessary without which social justice is a losing proposition. This was the fate of the great social experiments of the Soviet Union and China under Mao. Millions of people were sacrificed in the name of false ideologies and the utopias of forced socialist industrialization and forced collectivization built on the basis of those ideologies.

Social consciousness manifests itself in status group beliefs and in class confidence. We can evaluate instrumental rationality in the same way we evaluate distributive social justice. We have defined its ideal types. Now we need to define their empirical domains and indicators, and then proceed with their empirical evaluations. We can use the same statistical model of expanded normal distribution but with one difference. We will interpret its parameters as ideal types of rationality – of instrumental rationality for social consciousness and value-rationality for social conscience. Rationality in this sociological sense is directly related to democracy. For much of human history public policies have been decided by power-holders such as kings and monarchs who claimed divine license while the people were obliged to behave themselves. Freed from constrains of fight for power, participatory survey democracy can operate in the public interest by setting standards of substantive and formal value-rationality for social justice. The instrumental rationality of social consciousness that supports social conscience is another word for relative truth or falsehood.

We will model the ideal types of instrumental rationality by the same four parameters of expanded standard normal distribution using mean probit for facts; standard deviation for meaning; skewness for understanding, and kurtosis for interpretation. Similarly to skewness and kurtosis that combine certain characteristics of mean and standard deviation understanding and interpretation combine certain characteristics of interpenetrating facts and meanings. Applying this to our statistical model, we can attribute facts to the mean parameter; meaning to standard deviation; understanding to skewness and interpretation to kurtosis.

Status Beliefs and Class Confidence

Status group beliefs and class confidence are means for achieving social goals driven by the higher ideal of social justice. Taking the example of family status beliefs we define them operationally by cross-tabulating responses to survey questions about happiness in marriage and trust in people (Table 7-1). By this definition most Americans turn out to be family realists, i.e. belong to the medium-low group of family beliefs, while family optimists (medium-high status group) are in a minority. Family idealists and family pessimists are somewhere in the middle. They belong to the groups of the high and the low family status-conscious. Since the 1980's, the highest index of family status beliefs was in 1985-1988, during Ronald Reagan's time.

Operational Definition of Family Status Beliefs

Question 1 How happy is your marriage?
           (1) Very happy
           (2) Pretty happy
           (3) Not too happy
Question 2 Can most people be trusted or you can't be too careful in life?
           (1) Most can be trusted
           (2) Depends, DK, NA
           (3) You can't be too careful

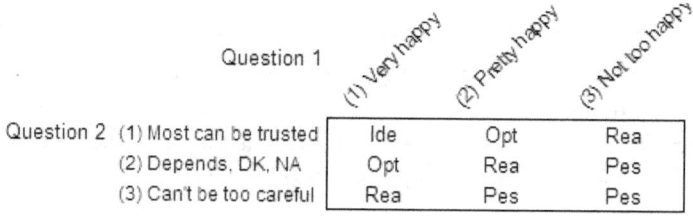

Question 2	(1) Very happy	(2) Pretty happy	(3) Not too happy
(1) Most can be trusted	Ide	Opt	Rea
(2) Depends, DK, NA	Opt	Rea	Pes
(3) Can't be too careful	Rea	Pes	Pes

Table 7-1. Operational definition of family status beliefs

We will therefore evaluate the current social structure of family beliefs using the 1985-1988 survey data as a standard. The statistical parameters of measuring the rationality of family beliefs align well with the meanings of the four ideal types of instrumental rationality – facts, meaning, understanding and interpretation – that are modeled by mean probit, its standard deviation, skewness and kurtosis. We find that the current structure of family status beliefs has an excessive surplus of mean, i.e. on facts at the expense of their interpretation (Table 7-2). Family happiness does not just happen. It is an act of will. There are pennies falling from heaven. But we still have to make an effort and pick them up.

	Reagan '85-'88		Obama '13-16		Deviation	Tolerated	Excessive	Instrumental rationality
Mean	0.70	24.5%	0.46	18.0%	6.5%	3.6%	2.8%	Facts
St deviation	0.68	23.9%	0.69	27.2%	-3.2%	-3.2%		Meaning
Skewness	0.57	19.9%	0.49	19.2%	0.8%	0.8%		Understanding
Kurtosis	0.90	31.6%	0.90	35.6%	-4.0%	-3.6%	-0.4%	Interpretation
Total	2.85	100.0%	2.53	100.0%	absTotal=>		3.20%	
Tolerance					3.6%			

Table 7-2 2013-2016 structure of family beliefs compared with 1985-1988

	Clinton '97-'00		Obama '13-16		Deviation	Tolerated	Excessive	Instrumental rationality
Mean	0.31	13.7%	0.20	10.2%	3.4%	3.4%	2.8%	0.6%	Facts
St deviation	0.71	31.6%	0.62	32.4%	-0.8%	-0.8%		Meaning
Skewness	0.44	19.8%	0.33	17.5%	2.3%	2.3%		Understanding
Kurtosis	0.78	35.0%	0.76	39.9%	-4.9%	-2.8%	-2.0%	Interpretation
Total	2.24	100.0%	1.91	100.0%	absTotal=>		2.60%	
Tolerance					2.8%			

Table 7-3 2013-2016 financial class confidence compared with 1997-2000

Moving on to class confidence, our data show a sharp rise in the proportion of financial pessimists in the USA after the financial crisis of 2008. Evaluating the instrumental rationality of current (2013-2016) financial class confidence by the high standard of 1997-2000, we find an excessive deficit in the kurtosis parameter, i.e. in interpretation (Table 7-3). This result is consistent with descriptive analyses of the time to the effect that the financial crisis of 2008 was due to financial overconfidence based on the misinformation spread by the banks regarding mortgage loan conditions and stock exchange quotes. The low level of class confidence following the crisis was a poor answer to the appeal asking "what you can to do for our country" rather than asking "what the country can do for you."

Class confidence and class preference mediate between prevailing class situations and class interests. The Marxist concept of class interest and class consciousness meant class antagonism. Max Weber advanced a different idea of socioeconomic commitment based on a study of North-European and American histories. He associated the achievements of the United States and the countries of northern Europe with the Protestant work ethic as the foundation of Western capitalism. As Weber saw it, it was this religious interest - named vocation or calling - and a rational worldly lifestyle of early ascetic Calvinist sects that brought about modern capitalism with all its successes in industry and commerce. Financial class preference is operationally defined by cross-tabulating responses to survey questions asking whether we spend too much or too little money on space exploration and on helping the poor (Table 7-4).

Operational Definition of Financial Class Preference

Question 1 Do you think we spend too much or too little money
      (1) Too little   on helping the poor?
      (2) About right
      (3) Too much
      (4) Don't know, NA

Question 2 Do you think we spend too much or too little money
      (1) Too little   on space exploration?
      (2) About right
      (3) Too much
      (4) Don't know, NA

	Question 1			
Question 2	(1) Too little	(2) About right	(3) Too much	(4) Don't know
(1) Too little	Str	Mod	Wea	No
(2) About right	Mod	Mod	Wea	No
(3) Too much	Wea	Wea	Wea	No
(4) Don't know, NA	No	No	No	No .

Table 7-4. Operational definition of financial class preference

To be sure, there was the other side of capitalism inspired by the same Protestant work ethic: exploitation of man by man so cogently exposed by Marxism. Weber saw this reality conceptualizing it as disenchantment of the world populated by "specialists without spirit, sensualists without heart." Atheistic communist morality did not fare any better however. The command economies of the socialist camp imploded eventually due in large measure to a lack of confidence in outdated communist ideals. We can use the idea of economic class preference corresponding to ends in action frame of reference – commitment to proportional social-structural harmony among all stratified social classes involved. In this sense class conscience spells commitment to class cooperation rather than to class antagonism and class struggle. The results of this analysis imply a reversal of excessive deviations from the standard of comparison as a matter of public policy.

Notes

[1] Habermas (1981).

8. Social Conscience: A Moral Compass

Social conscience is associated with conceptions of status group beliefs and class confidence. Status beliefs derive from status aspirations and follow them. Similarly, class confidence derives primarily from class interests in upward class mobility and follows such interests. Just like status position and status aspiration interpenetrate in status beliefs, so do the opposites of class situation and class interests interpenetrate in class confidence. This is what philosophers since Hume have been discussing as the impossibility of arriving at "ought" from "is." These two opposites were deemed irreconcilable.

The problem of mediating polar opposites was addressed by Hegel with his triadic dialectical scheme of *Aufhebung*. Sociology of action advances Hegel's solution by having two mediating members between opposites rather than one. In this double mutual cross-attribution the opposites penetrate one another producing mediation since the mediating elements carry the properties of both polar opposites.[1] Sociology is generally considered as a highly rational way of thinking about matters of public interest. However, it can also be seen as non-rational in the sense of making or not making ideals its primary subject-matter. We can speak of sociology as less rational if it takes reified social relations as its subject-matter – as in economics – rather than the ideals of fairness and rationality in social relations. The same consideration applies to the object of sociological studies, in our case to the goal-rationality of status desires and class preferences whose ideal types can be defined as pleasure, virtue, self-control and satisfaction.[2]

Do Ends Justify Means?

This problem of social conscience attributed to Machiavelli has raised a dispute that still continues to this day.[3] Is it ethical to steal money to buy medicine for a sick grandmother? Or conceal from the next of kin that his/her spouse has a terminal illness? Such dilemmas have puzzled philosophers for many years. The concept of value-rationality may help in answering these questions. Max Weber's distinction between instrumental and value-rationality of social action is based on the relationship between means and ideals or "ideal interests" as he called them. He associated instrumental rationality with social consciousness limited to estimates of means. By contrast, value-rationality was associated with social conscience that evaluated means in terms of values.[4] The ideal of value-rationality applies to evaluations of social conscience as the ideal of instrumental rationality applies to evaluations of social consciousness.

Philosophers of science tell us that theories are built from facts and concepts rather than from ideologies and their critiques. This is only partially true. While inductive grounded theories are indeed based on empirical data, their deductive sources are in the critical evaluations that happen to be dominant at a given time of history. In natural sciences these historic re-evaluations are called discoveries and "covering laws." Galileo's free fall, Newton's gravitation and Einstein's relativity are good examples.[5] These theories and their practical applications are considered rational and true since they incorporate conditions and ends of action.

So do ends justify means? As a general rule no. No ends can justify the means by themselves unless we mean a higher purpose, something that represents a social value, i.e. a purpose that is higher than the immediate one. Means can only be justified by a higher end. Thus social conscience involves a relationship means and ideals. It is wrong to kill, to steal and to bear false witness for personal gain. Yet soldiers in all armies are trained to kill, to steal and to lie for the higher purpose of a victory over an enemy. It all depends on how wide a community one identifies with. If you consider yourself to be a citizen of the world you will probably follow Kant's categorical imperative: "Act only according to that maxim whereby you can, at the same time, will that it should become a universal law."[6]

Such an argument applies to an individual unit act, an act that can only be attributed to individuals. If we want to transfer the same logic to groups and speak of collective consciousness and collective conscience we must associate the categories of means and ideals with categories of their empirical domains that have meaningful correspondences to the elements of the unit act. This is how the elements of unit act can serve as an action frame of reference. We find that for status groups the empirical domain of aspirations corresponds to ideals, in this case to the central ideal of distributive social justice, and the domain of beliefs to means.[7]

Having established these correspondences we can proceed with evaluations of collective conscience for status and class structures. We can illustrate empirically situations of collective "means" justified or not justified by evaluating structures of status beliefs and relevant status aspirations as representing means and ideals for status groups. The empirical structure of aspirations representing ideals will justify the structure of beliefs representing means only if it is found to be better than the structure of beliefs representing means. Collective "ideals" cannot justify collective "means" when their structure is found to be worse than that of the former. This is what gives us a moral compass orienting our social relations. Status beliefs can only be justified by status aspirations – not by desires. Similarly, class confidence can only be justified by class interests – not by class preferences.

It is owing to the unit act and its use as a frame of reference that we can know the relationships among social structures of status group aspirations and beliefs as well as those among class interests and class confidence. It is owing to this action frame of reference that we can do an analysis of empirical data that is firmly grounded in appropriate empirical domains where empirical indicators of abstract general concepts can be located. We do this by transferring the well-established relationships among the elements of the action frame of reference – conditions, ends, means and ideals – to the otherwise unrelated and chaotic elements of survey research data. As a result, raw survey data become indicators of status aspirations and class interests, or of status beliefs and class confidence.

Belief in providence may sustain us in situations of acute crisis, but normally it is belief in the improvement of family, income, educational and occupational status that is on our minds. In evaluating such status group beliefs we will speak of idealists, optimists, realists and pessimists as corresponding to high, medium-high, medium-low and low status group conscience. We can compare the rationality of status group beliefs to that of status aspirations, and then give a specific positive or a negative answer to the question whether these collective means are justified depending on the results of such empirical comparisons.[8]

Let us first compare the structure of occupational status beliefs to that of occupational status aspirations to distributive social justice. For the purposes of this analysis, idealistic, optimistic, realistic and pessimistic occupational beliefs are operationally defined as in a cross-tabulation of responses to two survey questions: (1) Do you believe people get ahead by hard work or they just get lucky? (2) How likely is it that you will lose your job within the next 12 months? Idealistic and optimistic status groups were assigned to those who sided with hard work and with not losing a job. Occupational status aspirations - strong, moderate, weak and absent – are defined as fairness in the social distribution occupational prestige scores.

A comparison of occupational status beliefs and aspirations shows that occupational aspirations have a lower sum total of their parameters. Therefore the answer to the dilemma of social conscience – whether to approve or disapprove the rationality of occupational beliefs will be negative. While the ends (occupational desires) never justify the means (occupational beliefs) by themselves, neither do the ideals in this case (Table 8-1). We will have to give a similar answer when comparing the social structures of educational aspirations and educational beliefs. The parameters of educational aspirations add educational beliefs. Educational aspirations are found to be less rational than educational beliefs. The answer to this dilemma of social conscience must be: the ideals do not justify the means in this case while ends never do (Table 8-2).

Class Confidence

For class structures the empirical domain of class confidence corresponds to means and class interest to ideals. Class preferences and class confidence mediate between the otherwise irreconcilable opposites of (generally unfair) class situations and class interests in upward social mobility. Class confidence becomes irrational when it becomes divorced from underlying class interests with a result that class preferences acquire lives of their own.

	Occupational beliefs		Occupat'l aspirations		Deviation	Excessive	Instrumental rationality
Mean	0.78	26.1%	0.75	25.8%	0.3%		Facts
Std. deviation	0.62	20.7%	0.67	23.0%	-2.3%	-0.8%	Meaning
Skewness	0.69	23.2%	0.59	20.4%	2.8%	1.2%	Understanding
Kurtosis	0.90	30.1%	0.90	30.8%	-0.7%		Interpretation
Total	3.00	100.0%	2.91	100.0%			
Tolerance					1.5%	2.1%	

Table 8-1. Occupational beliefs and aspiratons, 2013-2016

	Educational beliefs		Educational aspirations		Deviation	Excessive	Istrumental rationality
Mean	0.75	25.6%	0.44	18.8%	6.7%	2.2%	Facts
Std. deviation	0.67	22.7%	0.72	30.8%	-8.2%	-3.6%	Meaning
Skewness	0.59	20.2%	0.49	21.1%	-0.9%		Understanding
Kurtosis	0.93	31.5%	0.68	29.2%	2.3%		Interpretation
Total	2.94	100.0%	2.33	100.0%			
Tolerance					4.5%	5.8%	

Table 8-2. Educational beliefs and aspirations, 2013-2016

When this happens the delicate balance between prevailing class confidence and underlying class interests is disturbed and their integration breaks down as it happened in the financial crisis of 2008. That crisis was precipitated by exaggerated confidence in mortgage banking and investment operations with poorly understood super-complex financial instruments such as credit default swaps. It was appropriately described at the time as "irrational exuberance." Our empirical evaluations can demonstrate that the moral dilemmas of social class conscience, such as in budgeting and allocating national funds or in setting morally sensitive political programs, can have rational solutions.[9] With that in view let us compare the structure of environmental class confidence as representing means to that of environmental interests as ideals in the action frame of reference.

Environmental class confidence is defined operationally by cross-tabulating responses to the survey questions about levels of confidence in Congress and in the executive branch of US government. Environmental class interest is defined by responders indicating their opinion on whether we spend too much, too little or just enough for improving health care. Based on the analysis of their parameters, the structure of environmental class interests is found to be better than that of environmental confidence. The former justifies the latter (Table 8-3). There must be an opposite decision in the comparison of financial class interests and financial class confidence. The structure of financial class interests standing for ideals adds up to a higher sum total (Table 8-4).

	Environ'l confidence		Environ'l interest		Deviation	Tolerated	Excessive	Instrumental rationality
Mean	0.08	6.9%	0.72	25.6%	-18.7%	-14.6%	-4.1%	Facts
Std deviation	0.45	37.1%	0.65	23.1%	13.9%	13.9%		Meaning
Skewness	0.14	11.4%	0.62	21.9%	-10.5%	-10.5%		Understanding
Kurtosis	0.54	44.6%	0.83	29.4%	15.3%	14.6%	0.7%	Interpretation
Total	1.21	100.0%	2.83	100.0%		absTotal=>	4.8%	
Tolerance					14.6%			

Table 8-3. Environmental class confidence and interest, 2013-2016.

	Financial confidence		Financial interest		Deviation	Tolerated	Excessive	Instrumental rationality
Mean	0.20	10.2%	0.10	7.3%	3.0%	3.0%	3.0%	Facts
Std deviation	0.62	32.4%	0.48	35.1%	-2.7%	-2.7%		Meaning
Skewness	0.33	17.5%	0.16	11.3%	6.2%	4.6%	1.6%	Understanding
Kurtosis	0.76	39.9%	0.64	46.4%	-6.5%	-4.6%	-1.9%	Interpretation
Total	1.91	100.0%	1.37	100.0%		absTotal=>	3.5%	
Tolerance					4.6%			

Table 8-4. Financial class confidence and interest, 2013-2016

111

Rational Choice Theory

Status group desires and class preference can be empirically evaluated for their intensity irrespective of whether they are in favor or against the cause in question. Moral decisions of social status and class conscience in giving or not giving precedence to status desires and class preference over status beliefs and class confidence are also described as choice. The rationality of such choices is the subject matter of rational choice theory that highlights a simple yet seemingly versatile two-level model. The program of rational choice theory was designed for explaining outcomes of social structural changes as a way of bringing social theory and empirical research together.[10] Within its framework, outcomes of structural social changes are supposed to be explained by purposive actions of individuals who are guided by the rationality of making informed and optimal choices.

If action is characterized by the instrumental rationality of self-interest, it cannot be institutionally controlled and value-rational at the same time. And vice versa: if social conduct is value-rational and constrained by institutional norms, it cannot also be seen as self-interested instrumental action. Overall, the most serious charge against rational choice theory is that it is not capable of answering the big questions of sociology posed by the founders – Marx's question of social justice, Weber's question of rationalization, and Durkheim's question of social solidarity or cohesion.[11]

Various modifications have been proposed since Coleman's pioneering effort to meet these criticisms and to refine the original model of rational choice. In particular, it has been suggested that motivational assumptions of rational choice theory must include values without which this theory falls back on economists' narrow notion of subjective expected utility and overlooks the conceptual treasures of classical sociology.[12] A plea for more specific yet thick models of individual action was voiced in this connection – as in Weber - rather than general and thin ones that are substantively empty. But thick models can also be wrong if rational choice theory assumes wealth maximization as one of the leading motivational values of human behavior – unless such values are randomly distributed in a population.

A strong case has been proposed for using large-scale data-sets as explananda in rational action theory instead of case studies of the ethnographic kind. According to Goldthorpe while idiosyncratic effects of individual actions that are more often than not "uncertain, ambivalent, confused, or inconsistent" cancel each other out, the rationality of social actions aggregated in large data-sets would have explanatory power even if it was weak. Furthermore, deviations from rationality in such an analysis would be more telling than the rationality demonstrated in handpicked show cases of little substantive importance.[13]

There is no alternative to certain positivistic elements in a study of this kind where we take social data *comme les choses*, i.e. as things in Durkheim's sense. While improving such research and having an intense interest in a rigorous methodology of obtaining such facts, we must also recognize that at some point we will objectify them.

This is also expressed in the maxim that sociology can produce useful information for one-time use only, i.e. such that must be continuously updated. The post-structuralist research style assumes a passive reader for whom everything must be explained and who must thus be educated and empowered.[14] However, the burden is not on the writer. It is on the reader. The active reader has the option to challenge the writer, especially given today's Internet facilities. He can ask the writer to reveal his hidden interests and biases or else offer his own theories on this account.

Notes

[1] See Dubrovsky (2007).

[2] These categories go back to utilitarian philosophy of Jeremy Bentham and John Stuart Mill and further back to ancient Stoics' discussion of the purpose of life in their opposition to both Epicureans and Skeptics. The Stoic position has reached us via Cicero's "De officiis" and "De finibus bonum et malorum."

[3] See, for example, Balleck (1992).

[4] As his wife later reported, Weber saw his father's ethic as the ethic of success as opposed to his mother's ethic of conscience and responsibility (see Marianne Weber, 1975).

[5] See Hempel (1942).

[6] The second formulation of the categorical imperative is more personal: "Act in such a way that you treat humanity, whether in your own person or in the person of any other, never merely as a means to an end, but always at the same time as an end."

[7] As Dryzek (1989, p. 99) wrote, "Rationality is not a property of individuals but an aspiration of collectivities."

[8] Parsons' idea of dynamic structural-functional analysis was not too far removed from statistical path analysis except that he became immersed in its qualitative taxonomic-conceptual aspect developing a system of categories for motivational functions and those of social control. Writing in the middle of the 20th century, Parsons occasionally sounded very much like today's path analysts: "[The] essential feature of dynamic analysis in the fullest sense is the treatment of a body of *interdependent* phenomena simultaneously, in the mathematical sense. [...] The ideal solution is the possession of a logically complete system of dynamic generalizations which can state all the elements of reciprocal interdependence between all the variables of the system (Parsons 1954, pp. 215-216, emphasis in the original). Parsons did not believe an adequate mathematical apparatus existed for such research procedures, but his initial program envisaged systems of simultaneous equations and tests of (functional) significance (1954, pp. 215-218; 1951, pp. 21-22). Apparently, he did not know that Sewell Wright had proposed the idea of path analysis already in the 1920's.

[9] See Chase (1993), Paul (1959). Weber devoted the late portion of his creative life to the study of value-rationality looking for its empirical evidence in world religions while it is everywhere around us in mundane life.

[10] Coleman (1986, 1990).

[11] Ultee (1996).

[12] Hechter and Kanazawa (1997). While assuming consciously self-interested social action as producing social outcomes, many rational choice theories also talk about institutional constrains of action in the same breath. This assumption of normative institutional constraints is self-contradictory in that it presupposes value-rationality and social control that are opposites of self-interest.

[13] Goldthorpe (1996, 1998, 2007, pp. 117-189).

[14] Agger (1991).

9. Consistency of Institutional Structures

Gerhard Lenski's ideas of status crystallization and of status inconsistency as its opposite were found to be major sources of stress in society as well as in individuals and a breeding ground for radical movements of all kind.[1] By the late 1970's, after several critical opinions this idea was abandoned. Blalock and others pointed out to the identification problem in empirical research of status inconsistency meaning that causal effects of some of its several indicators acting together could not be attributed in a non-controversial way.[2] The subject-matter of status inconsistency did not die, however. It persisted in journalism under the name of "status–income disequilibrium" borrowing the language of economic science. The cases of status inconsistency cited in this connection were mainly between prestigious occupations and their relatively low remuneration, especially in members of creative trades and intellectuals. As for professional sociology, it did not return to this subject-matter. It fell out of fashion.

The theme of status and class inconsistency may not have been exhausted, though. In addition to income and occupational prestige that are the standard domains of social stratification and social mobility research in the tradition of Blau and Duncan, there are two more institutional domains where status inconsistency is also relevant: education and family. One reason these two domains have been less prominent in status inconsistency research may be because they are usually treated as independent variables affecting if not fully determining income and occupational status levels. Status inconsistency and "disequilibrium" are empirically found predominantly between occupational prestige and income – rather than income and education or income and family status. This is a good indication of a particular place occupied by these institutional domains in the system of their social stratification.

Evaluating Institutional Structures

The fact that educational and family institutional domains are considered less important than occupational and income ones means that they occupy lower positions in the stratified social system of institutional domains. This lesser importance was reflected in the way path analysis models were constructed in status attainment research. Once this question of hierarchy among institutional domains is settled, their social structures can be evaluated in the same way we evaluated distributive social justice. The difference will be that instead of structures of status groups and classes differentiated by institutional domains we will compare structures of institutional domains differentiated by levels of social status or class. All previously identified empirical indicators will remain the same. In this way we can isolate structures of institutional domains in status achievement without reducing the level of details in social differentiation.[3]

The normative aspect presumed by conditions of status inconsistency is that of parity or equality in status relations. We can therefore place this research area squarely into that of distributive social justice where, beside equality, the distributive principles of desert, claim-right and entitlement must also be considered. From this point of view the subject-matter of status consistency and inconsistency is but an aspect of the theme of distributive social justice. The difference is that instead of harmony in stratified structures of status groups differentiated by institutional domains and stages of status attainment or class formation processes, we evaluate the harmony of stratified elements of such processes differentiated by institutional domains and by levels of status groups and class stratification.

The identification problem is avoided in two ways. First, individual empirical indicators can be combined by cross-tabulating them as is done in this study where they serve as mutual controls. This makes it possible to split their joint distribution into one-dimensional levels of status or class hierarchy and attribute transformed unitary parameters of such social distributions to principles of distributive social justice. Secondly, the attribution of such effects is made possible by modeling major principles of distributive social justice on unitary statistical parameters of central tendency. Excessive deviations of these parameters from standards of comparison are then interpreted as surplus or deficit in the corresponding principles of distributive justice with obvious policy implications.

Income and Occupation

Comparing the structures of statistical parameters of achieved income and occupational status for the years 2013-2016 we in fact find that the American occupational social structure is of a much higher quality than that of income structure. The criterion for this judgment is the sum total of their parameters that is higher for occupation than for income. The deviations of the income structure from the occupational one are: an excessive deficit in Desert and an excessive surplus in Equality (Table 9-1). The level of the Equality principle in this structure is well within the limits of tolerance and can be ignored. This leads to the conclusion that the disparities between occupational prestige and income are not due to their inequality but rather due to the lack of assertiveness on the part of intellectual and other creative occupations as well as too much reliance on grants and other government entitlements. This is what the excessive deficits of Desert and Entitlement mean. A similar result is obtained when comparing the social structure of income to that of education. This comparison also shows that the American education relies too little on Desert and too much on Entitlement (Table 9-2).[4]

	Income status		Occupational status		Deviation	Tolerated	Excessive	Distributive justice
Mean	0.30	14.3%	0.75	25.8%	-11.5%	-6.2%	-5.3%	Desert
St.deviation	0.65	31.1%	0.67	23.0%	8.1%	6.2%	1.9%	Equality
Skewness	0.41	19.5%	0.59	20.4%	-0.9%	-0.9%		Claim-right
Kurtosis	0.73	35.1%	0.90	30.8%	4.3%	4.3%		Entitlement
Total	2.09	100.0%	2.91	100.0%		absTotal=>	7.2%	
Tolerance					6.2%			

Table 9-1. Structures of income and occupational status, 2013-2016

	Income status		Educational status		Deviation	Tolerated	Excessive	Distributive justice
Mean	0.30	14.3%	0.44	18.8%	-4.5%	-3.1%	-1.5%	Desert
St.deviation	0.65	31.1%	0.72	30.8%	0.3%	0.3%		Equality
Skewness	0.41	19.5%	0.49	21.1%	-1.6%	-1.6%		Claim-right
Kurtosis	0.73	35.1%	0.68	29.2%	5.8%	3.1%	2.8%	Entitlement
Total	2.09	100.0%	2.33	100.0%		absTotal=>	4.2%	
Tolerance					3.1%			

Table 9-2. Structures of income and educational status, 2013-2016

Status and Class Consistency

Institutional class structures are social structures of large-scale institutional domains rather than of specific institutions. If it is, for example, the institutional structure of financing or management we will speak of upper, middle and lower classes in these domains rather than specifically about banking or interest rates; or about business governance, or technostructure in Galbraith's sense;[5] we will speak about part-time workers or about the unemployed as employment classes rather than more specifically about the institutions of employment contract or collective bargaining. Surely such specification would be highly desirable, but it requires an inductive identification of concrete institutions out of their multitude in any single institutional domain. This task is beyond the present effort that is mostly methodological.

The deregulation of the banking industry in the 1990's was followed by high stock exchange activity and the rise in the living standards of young urban professionals. This is how changes of class structure can affect changes in social positions of status groups. We can compare these social structures using the same technique of estimating levels of excessive deviations from standards. This will allow us to determine levels of upward or downward social mobility of institutional status and class structures. Thus we find that the American structures of status group relations consistently fall behind structures of major institutional economic relations, in particular, behind environmental and employment ones (Tables 9-3 and 9-4).

	Environmental class		Family status		Deviation	Tolerated	Excessive	Distributive justice
Mean	0.72	25.6%	0.75	25.8%	0.2%	0.2%	0.2%	Desert
Std.deviation	0.65	23.1%	0.67	23.0%	-0.1%	-0.1%	-0.1%	Equality
Skewness	0.62	21.9%	0.59	20.4%	-1.5%	-0.8%	-0.7%	Claim-right
Kurtosis	0.83	29.4%	0.90	30.8%	1.4%	0.8%	0.6%	Entitlement
	2.83	100.0%	2.91	100.0%	absToral=>		1.3%	
					0.8%			

Table 9-3. Environmental class and family status structures, 2013-2016

	Employment class		Educational status		Deviation	Tolerated	Excessive	Distributive justice
Mean	0.68	24.1%	0.43	18.7%	5.4%	5.3%	0.2%	Desert
St deviation	0.59	21.0%	0.72	31.0%	-9.9%	-5.3%	-4.7%	Equality
Skewness	0.58	20.5%	0.49	21.1%	-0.6%	-0.6%		Claim-right
Kurtosis	0.97	34.4%	0.68	29.3%	5.1%	5.1%		Entitlement
Total	2.82	100.0%	2.32	100.0%	absTotal =>		4.9%	
Tolerance					5.3%			

Table 9-4. Educational status and employment class structures, 2013-2016

123

Similar results can be found in comparing the structures of achieved educational, occupational and income social status with employment, management and financial class structures. These imbalances and distortions of social harmony are major causes of a multitude of social problems. The policy implications in all these comparisons are clear. To avoid discovered deficiencies in status group and class structures their relevant excessive deviations must be reversed. Upward social mobility means more than improving structures of social status or class structures separately. Above all it resides in relationships between status and class, and it requires coordination and adjustments as a matter of public policy.

Analysis shows that sometimes social status structures lag behind class structures, as in the case of educational status and employment, and sometimes it is the other way around (Figure 6, Table 9-5). Max Weber described these changes as if they were made by a switchman who directs a country's development either on the rails of classes or the rails of status groups.

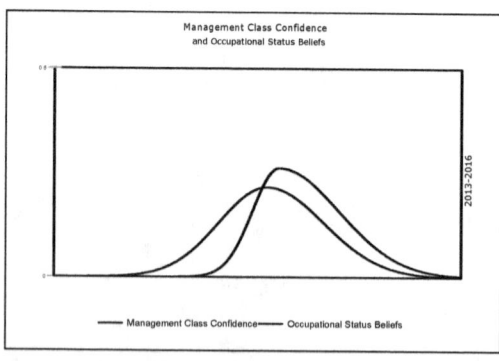

Figure 6. Management class confidence lags behind occupational status beliefs, 2013-2016.

Occupational Status Beliefs and Management Class Confidence, 2013-2016

	Occupatl beliefs		Management confce		Deviation	Excessive	Instrumental rationality
Mean	0.78	26.1%	0.64	23.5%	2.6%		Facts
Std.deviation	0.62	20.7%	0.71	26.0%	-5.3%	-2.4%	Meaning
Skewness	0.69	23.2%	0.54	20.0%	3.2%	0.3%	Understanding
Kurtosis	0.90	30.1%	0.83	30.6%	-0.4%		Interpretation
Total	3.00	100.0%	2.71	100.0%		2.8%	
Tolerance						2.9%	

Table 9-5. Occupational status beliefs lag behind management class cnfidence

However true this may have been in the past, we cannot now afford the luxury of sitting idly and trusting the pendulum of history to improve the situation for us. Public policies should focus on getting higher levels of status desires or class preference, of status beliefs or class confidence depending on which ones of them can legitimately be taken as standards of evaluation. The question is: which should be adjusted to which - status to class structures or class to status structures? This question is not for an ideological party line or for speculation as it is purely empirical. The answer depends on which of these types of social structures can legitimately serve as a standard of comparison.

These dependencies mean that better institutional structures will result in improved structures of status group relations, and vice versa, too. Distributive social justice works both ways. Its mechanisms of action can be sufficiently well revealed in what is sometimes denigrated as nonexperimental variable research. If distributions of stratified status groups show the same levels of fairness in joint distributions with stratified class structures of significant institutional domains we will find good relationships, e.g. indicated by correlations, within structures of status groups and in class structures separately as internal and external exchanges. In this way, we will find explanations of social exchanges across strata by exchanges of social values within social strata. We can thus explain structural mobility by circulation mobility and vice versa.

Besides social justice, there is also a long tradition of holding social equality as a moral imperative of normal social functioning and progressive development going back to Plato. Yet, Aristotle placed equality in the context of distributive justice. He conceived it as equality between two ratios that constitute a geometric proportion, not as that between men of unequal merits.[6] It is a challenge to translate these metaphors into procedures and techniques of quantitative social justice research. Social progress can be usefully conceived as a relative growth of higher strata and a reduction of lower ones with the assumption of a constant sum. The transition from general theory, or rather conceptualization, to such research is made possible by social indicators.

Notes

[1] Lenski (1953, 1954).

[2] Blalock (1966, 1967a, 11967b); Blalock and Riedesel (1978); Brown, Cretser and Lasswell (1988).

[3] Coleman (1986) points out that simple unity of purpose does not exist as a general case, but rather as a multitude of actions by actors pursuing their disparate goals. However, he does not make a clear distinction between institutional domains of social status and their empirical indicators such as lifestyle or orientation. All these are combined under the category of "configurations."

[4] The celebrated distributive principle of equality is within the limits of tolerance and is therefore not relevant here for policy decisions.

[5] Galbraith (1967).

[6] Quarrels and complaints come, Aristotle wrote, "when either equals have and are awarded unequal shares, or unequals equal shares" (*Nicomachean Ethics*, Book V).

10. The Time of Development

Social process and social structure are highly abstract notions, but their properties are always present in the more concrete ideas of spiral social development. Diachronic social development is a sequence of distinctive stages, a structured process, whereas synchronic social relations consist of recurring phases. It is a transforming structure, or process-in-structure. This is the locus of usually slow, secular social change that explodes in wars or civil strife if its natural course is artificially inhibited or precluded. Social reality combines elements of both structures and processes. Social development is not simply a process, but a structural process - a process of structures and a structure of processes. It is embodied primarily in the administration of social justice and rationality, and in demands of social as well as human rights to which social control – permissive or repressive - is a response.

It is useful to distinguish analytically between the abstractions of historic processes and social structures, on the one hand, and more concrete social movements, on the other, so as better to see their combinations in the meso-sphere. Typically social structures considered in social development will be those of institutions, and the processes will be those across the stages differentiated by social status desires and beliefs as well as by class preference and class confidence. This two-track social development is not to be confused with progress referring to the future rather than to the past. Desires and beliefs are always in the spiral time of development that combines features of both the linear time of status aspirations and the circular time of social conditions.

Liner, Circular and Spiral Time

Linear time is the time of change. Circular time is the time of the present, the time of repeating the same. In the natural world planets' revolutions around the sun are also seen in circular time. In human affairs both of these two kinds of time combine together in the spiral time of development which has properties of both circularity and linearity. Status aspirations and class interests exist in the linear time of change where every moment brings something new, something that has never existed before. Once they are achieved and realized, aspirations and interests find themselves in the circular time of repeating the same, or social reproduction. Circular time defines what we call social structures.

This is the time of seasons, but also the time of business as usual, of the status quo. The properties of both linear and circular time are combined in development in the form of advancing spiral motion. Development can be either evolutionary or revolutionary. In revolutionary development, time speeds up while structures of space narrow down. In medical practice interpretation of symptoms speeds up as the circle of possible diagnoses narrows. By contrast, in evolutionary development time slows down while structures of space expand. The process of successful medical treatment slows down as the range of recovery indicators expands. In a similar vein, economists explain the high value of diamonds compared to much more useful water by the rarity of diamonds, i.e. by the narrowing down of the opportunities of finding them. Its opposite, the slowing down of business activity with an expansion of its range is known in economics as the law of diminishing marginal utility of return.

Social differentiation is found at the intersection of two abstract sociological notions: social statics and social dynamics, or social structure and process. Pure social process, or history, can be differentiated by its component trends. However, since historic trends are of different strength and duration, their contemporary view never presents a complete or coherent picture. Their relevance for the present is only revealed in the static, structural view. Lacking any specificity beyond extant social injustices, this purely structural view is likewise but a useful abstraction. It is in this sense that status groups and social classes as pure relations of social hierarchy become the most abstract cross-sectional structural dimension of social differentiation. A further differentiation of status groups and classes into institutional domains provides a much more accurate picture of social stratification.

In development we look for a process in structures. In progress, on the contrary, we build structures out of a process. At each stage of development, certain (statistical) elements of structures change more than others. But small changes may also be important. We can speak of slow or fast development but also of gain or loss of its certain elements. This is where process and structure combine in structural process, as an interpenetrating combination of both. In classical mechanics, this is energy (gravitation, electromagnetic force, strong and weak nuclear forces). Einstein's $e=mc^2$ means that progress is an acceleration of mass. Our maximal value of one in relative estimates on the scale of zero to one is what corresponds to Einstein's speed of light as the maximal speed in nature.

If we consider "space" in structural terms, then it will have a plurality of dimensions – at least four: A, B, aB, and bA. Time (or process) will also have the same four dimensions (beginning, end, and two middle terms: beginning of the end, and the end of the beginning - as invoked famously by Churchill). The dimensions of social space are: low, high, lower-middle, and upper-middle, or else nearness, distance, near distance, further proximity. These dimensions have often been conceived as Earth, heaven, heaven on earth, and downfall from heaven. In short, the dimensions of time and space can be viewed in other than Cartesian terms. This is based on an imagery stretching out extensively. Rather, it is time that is extensive in which space is intensive. The tree-dimensional model of space is based on Cartesian geometry. Actually both have four dimensions. We know very little about the early history (or pre-history) of humanity and equally very little about its future. Our knowledge is mostly based on the intermediate time between distant past and future. Time is curved indeed in this sense. Did Einstein assume straight linear time?

Social Time and Space

If time and space are put as abscissa and ordinate in the Cartesian diagram, then development will be a collection of points in the intersection of both time and space values. Time and space combine to form temporal space and spatial time. This is why social space is seen as both expanding (the opposite of centralization) and extending (the opposite of concentration). Development is akin to physical motion. Its destination is not a point, however, but a structure. Arrival at a destination is usually more important than departure. Both process and structure have directionality. The social analog of this is social mobility. Our standard of consistency in development is like Einstein's observer – located somewhere between the point of departure and the point of arrival. Progress is like going; development, like coming. Edward Bernstein said appropriately in this sense, "The movement is everything, its final result, nothing." Destination and departure are real, not just extrapolated or interpolated.

Retrospective development toward a known point in the past – whether distant or near past – is not to be confused with prospective images of progress as part of utopian thinking. Future social conditions are created by social action and its collective analogues. They are only partly dependent on the past. If development can be fast or slow, progress (and social decline, too) can be either accelerated or delayed. Progress is measured by acceleration; development, by speed. We need to reduce a series of social structures to one. This is what combining process and structure means. These days time and space are also known as process and structure. These system-structural terms were used initially in biology, and then accepted as a general scientific conception.

The magnitudes of restraining social control are equal in size and opposite in sign to excessive deviations of indicator proportions, i.e., deviations beyond tolerated ones. Such control reverses the surplus or deficit of statistical structural parameters and in this way, of the distribution of values for social strata only in part. The remaining deficits are covered by harmonizing social control that debits, as it were, other social strata having remaining surpluses of values. An index of rectificatory justice varying from zero to one is obtained as a balance of subtracting specific absolute deviations of restraining and harmonizing social control. Specific absolute deviations of restraining and harmonizing control are defined as total absolute restraining and total absolute harmonizing control divided by their respective maximal limits.

Deviations are better measured from certain previous points in time, i.e. as in time series. The effect must be stronger for more recent time points and weaker for more distant ones, for example, as a moving average with different factors, e.g. ARIMA. This would account, among other things, for two-term presidencies that highlight the differences from predecessors. But we could also simply be historically specific. Except that this would imply intentionality and action that more properly belongs to a specific empirical domain as a social indicator in its own right. For process and developmental analysis proportions must be adjusted to row averages. These averages can be interpreted as either extrapolations (forecasts) or interpolations (origins) of the process or development under consideration.

There is no such thing as underdevelopment. What is meant by this term is lack of progress and/or slow development, or even decline. All current social systems are in their particular states of local development so long as they have a history. Development is always retrospective, only progress is prospective. We begin by modeling processes and structures separately, then combine them together. The processes can be seen as currents. We can speak about the magnitude of change and the magnitude of constancy in a process, and then combine these two measures with the weights of the golden section. This is the measurement of social history. The biggest change in development (or process, for that matter) can be described as significant or important for a particular period of time. It can always be identified by the biggest change in any of the four parameters – Desert, Equality, Claim-right or Entitlement - and that period can acquire its identity according to that change. Social developmental differences are not so much in the changes of frequencies (these are outer manifestations only), but rather in their distributions as measured by our four parameters: mean probit, standard deviation, skewness, and kurtosis.

If process is conceived as constant change and structure as unified plurality, development becomes unified plurality in constant change. The difficulty is to define the abstract notion of development operationally. As a structural social process, development means a process involving several status and class structures. In natural sciences the order is the opposite: it goes from structure to process.[1] In contrast to linear sequences of social development that are responsible for relatively stable but ever changing social institutions, the artifacts of cyclical social differentiation can erode and be obliterated much more quickly unless they are continuously regenerated, reproduced and reconfirmed.

Measuring Development

The categories of social differentiation are revealed in the evolution of social space and social time.[2] To overcome the historicist confusion between factually concrete situational history having no evolutionary logic of its own and formal reconstructions of social evolution guided by a logic of abstract conceptual schemes, it is necessary to abandon attempts of finding social evolution in changes of stratified social structures that are always accidental byproducts of purposeful social development.

Instead, reconstructions of social evolution should be confined only to structural processes that civilization has been appropriating and improving in its material environment – social space and time. If we additionally assume interplay of multiple institutional avenues in the evolution of human social environment, we can also overcome prevailing skepticism about the possibility of progressive development that originated in the demise of the 19th-century ideas of linear and providential history as conceived by Comte, among others. It is also useful to distinguish in this connection between cognitive and objectified meanings of this evolution. While we speak of sequential evolutionary stages as markers of linear differentiation of institutional domains in a strictly objectified sense of existing stock of knowledge, the evolution of social space and time responsible for differentiation must be considered in both its cognitive and objectified senses since it is a less studied topic.

We need to promote regular surveys, especially the ones that deal with social and economic issues in sufficient depth – rather than just straw polls serving electoral political purposes. Then, we need to see that such surveys are properly funded. And lastly, we need to see that survey data are properly analyzed. A constitutional amendment would be helpful to institutionalize this kind of survey analysis to serve as a competitor to congressional work. Thus conceived, participatory survey democracy will not be confused with the liberal democracy of protests, strikes, social movements, and other acts opposing representative government policies.

It is possible to conceive of social structures as momentary cross-sectional views of social processes involving ever-changing relative positions of significant social groups and classes reproduced in the changing relative strengths and successes of social movements that are supported actively or passively. Yet these are just useful analytical abstractions. Concrete realities of any society reside in the intermediate meso-sphere of transitions between these two mutually exclusive macro and micro perspectives. Concrete social reality combines elements of both of these two perspectives. It is embodied primarily in government, or in social control, as administration of social justice and rationality, and in demands of social as well as human rights to which social control is a response. Such conceptions of historic processes and social structures help us see better their combinations in the meso-sphere.

While retrospective social development can be seen as consisting of transitions between successive structures of social injustice, it is also a product of a multitude of social movements pursuing their causes, albeit often conflicting ones. If social injustices inherent in all real societies are mirrored in deviations from the norm of rationality designed to rectify them, why do some movements gain strength and support, grow, become organized and institutionalized, while others lose strength and withering away? If the destructive potential of conflicting social movements is counterbalanced by values of social justice that help restore social cohesion - or social solidarity - why do some societies succeed and others fail?

To answer these questions, we must take into account the fact that deviations from rationality can be either tolerable or excessive. Hence, we must assume that normal restraining social control channels social forces entangled in excessively unjust social structures back into the sphere of tolerable deviations by achieving more equitable and more rational structures of valued social resources. By contrast, permissive social control fails to rectify even excessive social injustices while repressive social control attempts to rectify even tolerable ones. It for these reasons primarily that any society and any civilization, no matter how successful in the past, can fail and disintegrate if the imperatives of social justice and rationality are not met.

Notes

[1] Durkheim wrote in his sense, "[... When] one undertakes to explain social phenomenon the efficient cause which produces it and the function it fulfills must be investigated separately. We use the word 'function' in preference to 'end' or 'goal' precisely because social phenomena generally do not exist for the usefulness of the results they produce" (1982, p.123).

[2] Popper (1986, pp. 151, 158) warned about considering historic processes without the structural aspects of development: "Historicism mistakes [...] interpretations for theories. This is one of its cardinal errors. [...] The human factor is the ultimate uncertain and wayward element in social life and in all social institutions. [... Every] attempt at controlling it completely must lead to tyranny; which means, to the omnipotence of the human factor - the whims of a few men, or even of one."

References

Agger, Ben. (1991). Critical Theory, Poststructuralism,
    Postmodernism: Their Sociological Relevance. *Annual
    Review of Sociology*, Vol. 17, pp. 105-131.
Berger, Peter L., and Thomas Luckmann. (1967). *The Social Construction
    Of Reality: A Treatise in the Sociology of Knowledge*. Garden City,
    NJ: Doubleday.
Blalock, Hubert M. Jr. (1966).The Identification Problem and Theory
    Building: The Case of Status Inconsistency. *American
    Sociological Review*, Vol. 31, No. 1 (Feb.), pp. 52-61.
_____(1967). Status Inconsistency, Social Mobility, Status
    Integration and Structural Effects. *American Sociological Review*,
    Vol. 32, No. 5 (Oct.), pp. 790-801.
Blau, Peter M., and Otis Dudley Duncan. (1967). *The American
    Occupational Structure*. New York: Wiley.
Blocker, T. Jean and Paul L. Riedesel. (1978). The Nonconsequences
    of Objective and Subjective Status Inconsistency: Requiem
    for a Moribund Concept. *The Sociological Quarterly*, Vol. 19,
    No. 2 (Spring), pp. 332-339.
Bourdieu, Pierre and Loic J. D. Wacquant. (1992). An *Invitation
    to Reflexive Sociology*. University of Chicago Press.
Brown, Peter G. (1976). Ethics and Policy Research. *Policy Analysis*,
    Vol. 2, No. 2, pp. 325-340
Brown, Wayne Curtis; Gary A. Cretser; Thomas E. Lasswell. (1988).
    Measuring Status Inconsistency: More Trouble than It's
    Worth? *Sociological Perspectives*, Vol. 31, No. 2 (Apr.), pp. 213-
    237.
Chan, Tak Wing and John H. Goldthorpe. (2004). Is There a Status
    Order in Contemporary British Society? *European Sociological
    Review*, 20, pp. 383-401.
_____ (2007). Social Status and Newspaper Readership. *American
    Journal of Sociology*, 112(4), pp. 1095-1134.
Chase, James (1993). The American Conscience. *World Policy Journal*,
    Vol. 10, No. 3, pp. 111-112.

Cicourel, Aaron V. (1973). *Cognitive Sociology: Language and Meaning in Social Interaction.* London: Penguin.

Dryzek, John S. (1989). Policy Sciences of Democracy. *Polity.* Vol. XXII, No. 1, p. 99.

Dubrovsky, Vitaly. (2004). Toward system principles: general system theory and the alternative approach. *System Research and Behavioral Science,* 21(2), pp. 109-122.

Durkheim, Emile. (1982). *The Rules of Sociological Method and Selected Texts of Sociology and Its Method.* New York: Free Press.

Gadamer, Hans-Georg. (1985). *Rhetoric, Hermeneutics, and the Critique of Ideology. The Hermeneutic Reader.* Pp. 274-292. New York: Continuum.

_____. (1988). *Truth and Method.* New York: Crossboard.

Galbraith, John Kenneth. (1967). *The New Industrial State.* New York: Signet.

Giddens, Anthony. (1984). The Constitution of Society: Outline of the Theory of Structuration. Berkeley and Los Angeles: University of California Press.

Gonzalez, Servando. (2010). *Psychological Warfare and the New World Order.* California: Spooks Books.

Habermas, Jurgen. (1979). *Communication and Evolution of Society.* Boston: Beacon Press.

_____. (1981). *The Theory of Communicative Action. Volume One. Reason and the Rationalization of Society.* Boston: Beacon Press.

_____. (1985). On Hermeneutics' Claim of Universality. *Rhetoric, Hermeneutics, and the Critique of Ideology. The Hermeneutic Reader.* Pp. 294-319. New York: Continuum.

Hempel, Karl. (1942). "The Function of General Laws in History," *Journal of Philosophy,* Vol. 39, pp. 35–48.

Keynes, John Maynard. (1964). *General Theory of Employment, Interest, and Money. New York:* Harcourt Brace & Company.

Lenski, Gerhard E. (1954). Status Crystallization: A Non-Vertical Dimension of Social Status. *American Sociological Review,* Vol. 19, No. 4 (Aug.), pp. 405-413.

_____ (1956). Social Participation and Status Crystallization. *American Sociological Review,* Vol. 21, No. 4 (Aug.), pp. 458-464.

Luhmann, Niklas. (1982). *The Differentiation of Society.* New York: Columbia University Press.

Michels, Robert. (1962). Political Parties: A Sociological Study of the Oligarchial Tendencies of Modern Democracy. New York: Free Press.

Balleck, Barry J. (1992). When the Ends Justify the Means: Thomas Jefferson and the Louisiana Purchase. *Presidential Studies Quarterly*, Vol. 22, No. 4, pp. 679-696.

Parsons, Talcott. 1951. *The Social System*. New York: Free Press.

———. 1954. *Essays in Sociological Theory. Revised Edition*. New York: Free Press.

———. (1968). *The Structure of Social Action*. New York: Free Press.

Pateman, Carole. (1970). *Participation and Democratic Theory*. Cambridge University Press.

——— (2012). APSA Presidential Address: Participatory Democracy Revisited. *Perspectives on Politics*, Vol. 10, No. 1, pp. 7-19.

Paul, Julius (1959). The Supreme Court: Mirror of the American Conscience. *The American Journal of Economics and Sociology*, Vol. 19, No. 1, pp. 1-15.

Polanyi, Karl. (1944). *The Great Transformation*. Boston: Beacon Hill.

Popper, Karl. (1986). *The Poverty of Historicism*. London: Ark.

Rawls, John. (1999). *A Theory of Justice. Revised Edition*. Cambridge, MA: Harvard University Press.

Robinson, Joan. (1965) *The economics of imperfect competition*. London: Macmillan.

Samuelson, Paul A. (1976). *Economics*. London: McGraw Hill.

Schumpeter, Joseph A. (1974). *Capitalism, Socialism and Democracy*. Third edition. New York: Harper Colophon Books.

Smikun, Emanuel. (2004). Valuable Objects and Their Differentiation in Social Space and Time. *Fast Capitalism* Vol.1, 1.

Sorokin, Pitirim A. (1959). *Social and Cultural Mobility*. New York: Free Press.

——— (1947). *Society, Culture and Personality: Their Structure and Dynamics. A System of General Sociology*. New York: Harper and Brothers.

Verba, Sidney. (1996). The Citizen as Respondent: Sample Surveys and American Democracy Presidential Address, American

Political Science Association, 1995. *The American Political Science Review.* Vol. 90, No. 1 (Mar.), pp. 1-7.

_____ (2003). Would the Dream of Political Equality Turn out to Be a Nightmare? Perspectives on Politics, Vol. 1, No. 4 (Dec.), pp. 663-679.

Weber, Marianne. (1975). *Max Weber: A Biography.* New York: John Wiley.

Weber, Max (1978). *Economy and Society. An Outline of Interpretive Sociology.* Berkeley, CA: University of California Press.

Winters, Jeffrey A. and Benjamin I. Page (2009). Oligarchy in the United States? *Perspectives on Politics*, Vol. 7, pp. 731-732.

Name Index